SACRED
RITUALS

SACRED RITUALS

Connecting with Spirit through Labyrinths, Sand Paintings & Other Traditional Arts

Eileen London & Belinda Recio

FAIR WINDS
PRESS
GLOUCESTER, MASSACHUSETTS

Text © 2004 Eileen London & Belinda Recio
First published in the USA in 2004 by
Fair Winds Press
33 Commercial Street
Gloucester, MA 01930

Library of Congress Cataloging-in-Publication Data

Recio, Belinda, 1961-
  Sacred rituals : creating labyrinths, sand paintings, and other spiritual art / Belinda Recio
& Eileen London.
       p. cm.
Includes bibliographical references and index.
  ISBN 1-59233-050-9
  1. Ritual. 2. Rites and ceremonies. I. London, Eileen. II. Title.
  BL600.R433 2004
  203'.8--dc22

                                                                        2003021277

10 9 8 7 6 5 4 3 2

Cover design by Belinda Recio
Book design by Belinda Recio & True North Productions

Printed and bound in China

Every effort has been made to ensure that all the information in this book is accurate. However, due to differing conditions and other variables, the publisher and authors cannot be held responsible for any injuries, losses, and other damages that may result from the use of information in this book.

"True friendship between two human beings exists only when there is a third friend present: Call this third friend God, or dharma, or simply the sacred."

—Philip Zaleski and Paul Kaufman,
Gifts of the Spirit

We dedicate this book to our ever-present third collaborator.

Acknowledgments

Warm and heartfelt thanks to everyone who helped us with this book, most especially to Eric Workman, our photographer, for his talents, resourcefulness, and generosity.

We are also very grateful to the following people and their associated organizations for their knowledge, guidance, and reviews of our text: Kaji Aso, Kate Finnegan, and Kaji Aso Studio and Institute for the Arts, Boston, MA; Michael LaFosse, Richard Blase, and Origamido, Haverhill, MA; Patricia Vesey-McGrew, President of the C. G. Jung Institute, Boston, MA; Joan Wilcox, author and lecturer on the sacred Andean traditions; and Julie Moir Messervy, garden designer, author, and lecturer.

Special thanks, also, to William Johnston for his production and design guidance; to Stephanie Hobart and Sacred and Folk Gallery, Gloucester, MA; to St. Andrews Episcopal Church, Marblehead, MA; to Duke Klauk and Ten Thousand Waves, Santa Fe, NM; to Toby Evans and The Prarie Labyrinth; to Kristin Mills for her versatile artistic talents; to Susan Weeks for her photograph; to the Class of 2004 at the Cape Ann Waldorf School in Beverly Farms, MA, for making and hanging prayer flags with us; to Terry Sivili, Drepung Loseling Monastery, and the Mystical Arts of Tibet; to Sarah Walsh, and to Peter Trefry, for walking the sand labyrinth on Singing Beach.

Our very special thanks to Lynne Havighurst for helping us find our way to Fair Winds Press; to our agent, Cathy Sigmon, for all of her support, and to Holly Schmidt and Fair Winds Press for believing in this book.

Finally, we would like to express our deepest gratitude to our friends and families, most especially to Ed Blomquist from Belinda and to Kennan Masters from Eileen.

Authors' Note

We came to write this book as the result of our personal explorations of rituals and the experiences they have brought to each of our lives. For this reason we wrote the book in our own voices, letting our stories and commentary remain in the first person singular.

Although each of us was primarily responsible for specific sections of the text, we elected not to attribute these sections to one or the other of us. Having written together before, we knew that the collaborative process requires a certain amount of "disappearing" into each other's words. Therefore we were concerned less with the genesis of the words than with the shared process of transforming them into the book that you hold in your hands.

Collaboration, like ritual, is a blending of the personal and the communal, a merging of individual lives and shared human experience. The heart and soul of collaboration rests in the truth that the whole really is greater than the sum of its parts.

CONTENTS

Facing page: Ten Thousand Waves, Santa Fe, New Mexico

Introduction

When we engage in ritual, we address our need to feel connected—to ourselves, each other, and the world. The word "religion," so strongly associated with ritual, originates in a word meaning "to bind together." Ritual—the language of religion—binds us to the whole of creation, and it is in this bond that we can encounter the sacred. Ritual works through its two-fold nature. Labyrinth walking, sand painting, and every other ritual ever created have two essential aspects in common: intention and action, or "heart and hand." The "intention" is the purpose of the ritual—it's the object for which the action is offered. One's intention for taking a pilgrimage might be to find meaning at every crossroad, whereas the intention behind raking sand in a *karensansui* meditation garden might be to achieve the Zen state of no-mind. The "action" of the ritual is what one actually does, such as travel, rake the sand, and so on. It's the symbolic action sanctified by personal faith or spiritual tradition.

The two aspects of ritual—heart and hand, or intention and action—work together to focus our minds on the implications of what we are doing. By acting out our intentions, we feel them more completely—in body, mind, and soul. When Tibetan Buddhist monks take days to create an exquisite mandala of colored sand and then scatter it upon completion, they are acting out an intention to accept the impermanence of all things. How much more heartfelt is the realization of impermanence after one sweeps up a work of art that took days to create! Likewise, when a Japanese tea master pays attention to every detail associated with preparing and serving tea, he enacts the greatness of little things and the sacredness of simple acts in ways that demand his complete presence and participation.

When humans participate in ceremony, they enter a sacred space. Everything outside of that space fades in importance. Time takes on a different dimension. Emotions flow more freely. The bodies of participants become filled with the energy of life, and this energy reaches out and blesses the creation around them. All is made new; everything becomes sacred.

—Sun Bear

So, by acting out our intentions we pay attention to both what we are doing and why, and we become fully present in the moment. This quality of being, called "mindfulness" in the Buddhist tradition, is a type of focused concentration. In many modes of consciousness, the ego acts as the barrier that keeps us separated from our "true" self, others, and the world. In a state of mindfulness, however, the ego barrier dissolves and we merge with the moment. Being fully present allows us to find that place within ourselves where we can encounter the divine. Many spiritual traditions believe that to experience God, the energy of creation, or a higher consciousness, we first need to be present and pay attention. Ritual can help us to do that—to center in the moment so that we might, as William Blake wrote, "see a world in a grain of sand and eternity in an hour."

Ritual, then, is the journey; the sacred is the destination. Just as there are many different roads to any destination, there are many rituals that can lead us to the sacred. In this book, we present fourteen rituals, representing roads to the sacred from a diversity of spiritual traditions. The book is divided into three sections: *Creating Sacred Space*, *Ways to the Center*, and *The Path of Prayer*. In the first section, *Creating Sacred Space*, we explore different approaches to creating what ancient Greek philosophers

called *temenos*, a sanctuary in which we feel our connection with spirit. The second section, *Ways to the Center*, presents rituals that help us to focus and be present in the moment. The last section, the *Path of Prayer*, celebrates the wisdom of the apostle Paul, who said that prayer can take any form as long as it comes from the heart. Each chapter is devoted to one ritual and includes an overview of the traditions that gave rise to it and instructions or suggestions for ways to engage in it. Some chapters have specific instructions, such as how to make a smudge stick; others present open-ended suggestions for how you might use a ritual in your life, such as making travel sacred by turning it from a "trip" into a "pilgrimage." The instructions and suggestions are open to personal adaptation, and we encourage you to make each ritual your own by bringing your faith, creativity, and talents to it.

Although most of the rituals in this book originate in specific spiritual traditions, you do not need to belong to a particular faith in order to participate in them. Rituals are only paths to the sacred—they are not the sacred itself. You need not fear that you are dishonoring a particular culture's ritual by making it your own. Many religious scholars believe that we are at the beginning of an interspiritual age, a time when spiritual diversity will lead to a commonality of spiritual values. It is in this spirit of interfaith—in which the Buddha mind can manifest while walking a labyrinth, Christ can be experienced in a tea ceremony, and the light of Allah can appear in a candle flame—that we wrote this book.

As a spiritual philosophy that honors the wisdom of all spiritual traditions, Interfaith is a relatively new paradigm. However, the assimilation of beliefs is as ancient as religion itself. New religions often embody vestiges of indigenous beliefs, as seen in these "spirit houses" built by Theravada Buddhists in Laos. The Buddhist Lao honor pre-Buddhist animist spirits by building elaborate miniature dwellings on which they place offerings of incense, spices, flowers, and food.

BE SOFT IN YOUR PRACTICE.

Think of the method as a fine silvery stream,

not a raging waterfall. Follow the stream,

have faith in its course. It will go its own way,

meandering here, trickling there. It will find

the grooves, the cracks, the crevices.

Just follow it. Never let it out of your sight.

It will take you.

—*Sheng-yen*

PART ONE

Creating
Sacred Space

At the Threshold Between
Heaven and Earth
ALTARS

To experience the sacred is to connect with the deeper meaning of life and surrender to a higher presence. The sacred can manifest anywhere and in any way—it can unfold in a quiet canyon or burst forth in joyous gospel singing. Thoreau called the sacred "the divine energy everywhere," and the Tao-te Ching describes the sacred as "hidden but always present." One way we connect with this unseen, soul-nourishing force is to invite it into our hearts through the altar.

At this moment I am sitting at my desk, writing by hand. My desk has always been a type of altar for me. I sit here to think, write, meditate, and sometimes pray. On the edge of my desk, against the wall, are my altar objects: a small sculpture of a winged dog called the "Guardian of Hopes and Dreams" that my husband gave me; an antique domino with seven dots, because seven has always been a sacred number for me; a collection of bear and wolf fetishes, because bears are associated with healing and the wolves—a symbol of the wild spirit—were a gift from a dear friend; a fossilized spiral ammonite shell that represents life's simultaneous journey inward and outward; a ceramic thimble from my grandmother; a journal; a box filled with incense, herbs, and sealing wax; tiny dried red roses in a sea-green ink bottle that I discovered in my backyard the day I moved into my house; and several other objects of personal meaning and faith. On the wall above my desk is a bulletin board papered with photos of loved ones, poems, an origami crane, a few watercolors painted by my sister on scraps of corrugated cardboard, my deceased uncle's medal of honor, and my mother's timeworn paper protractor from fifty years ago. This arrangement of objects creates a very intimate kind of

sacred space, one that helps me center and connect with my own journey and those who have been part of it.

From a functional perspective, an altar is a structure that serves as the center of a ceremony. On it, offerings are made, incense is burned, and objects are consecrated. In the space created by an altar, prayer, meditation, healing, and other acts of faith are practiced. Symbolically, the altar bridges the boundary between heaven and earth—it is a threshold between the world of matter and the world of spirit. For this reason, altars are often constructed in cemeteries, at the edge of forests, and on river banks—the borderlands between life and death, darkness and light, this world and the next. There, at the boundary between the material and spiritual worlds, we make altars so that we can encounter the sacred.

We seem to share an unconscious urge to create altars—it's part of what makes us human. In fact, ever since we first sensed the mysterious force that animates life, we've erected altars to honor and appease it. The Neanderthals, who lived over 75,000 years ago, made altars, and we're still making them today, even if they are little more than unconsciously created tableaus adorning our homes and workspaces. Our altars continue to express our need to connect with an unseen force, one that inspires us to give it form. So we build a cathedral, place a statue of Buddha in a garden sanctuary, or arrange talismans and souvenirs next to photographs of loved ones. Altar objects, whether a shell, Torah, bear fetish, or St. Francis figure, evoke emotion in us. Altars conjure the sacred because they stimulate our imaginations, provoking us to go beyond surface appearance to the deeper meanings that resonate in our hearts.

A cave altar in Laos

This richly decorated Hindu altar has a series of folding doors that symbolically suggest a progression from the outer world to the inner.

*Settle yourself
in solitude
and you will
come upon
God in yourself.*
—Teresa of Avila

Inside the Basilica of Notre Dame, Montreal, Quebec

Objects of Power: Talismans and Amulets

In ancient times, our ancestors perceived everything as alive with spirit, including objects that most of us now perceive as inanimate, such as stones, feathers, shells, and bones. Because everything seemed animate and had the potential to possess power, early humans created "power objects" to help them interact with the world—to protect themselves from negative forces and to attract positive forces. But power objects aren't just relics from the past—they are still used today. Known by names such as talismans, amulets, fetishes, and charms, power objects are natural or cultural items that are imbued with symbolic meaning and power by the person or culture that uses them. The power behind such an object is the faith of the person interacting with it, whether that faith be in the power of a Roman Catholic saint, a Buddhist relic, a Zuni mountain lion fetish, or a stone found on a beach. The power of the human spirit works through the object. If an object comforts us or gives us hope, that comfort or hope can change the way we act, which can potentially change the outcome of a particular situation, or even, sometimes, the course of one's life.

Making an Altar

Altars are often spontaneously assembled, as if the invisible presence of the sacred somehow stimulates an unconscious urge to create them. If you look around your home or even your workspace, you probably already have altar-like groupings of meaningful objects and photographs. Once you decide to make an altar, the process may unfold entirely on its own, without much thinking on your part. However, making an altar can be a ritual of soulful creativity in which you connect with your imagination and your spiritual center. To this end, we've included the following suggestions and questions to help guide you through the ritual.

Look around your home and you will probably find altar-like groupings of meaningful objects.

What You Need

Altar objects should relate to the intention of your altar, and they should engage your senses and evoke emotion. Your objects might be religious in nature, or they could be keepsakes, sacred souvenirs, charms, talismans, stones, shells, candles, incense, or flowers. Even ordinary objects can have profound meaning. Consider a shell you found on your favorite beach the morning someone close to you passed away, or a stone shaped like a heart found along a river's edge the day before you met your partner. You might also want to use a cloth to cover the surface of your altar.

Identify the Purpose of Your Altar

Before you make your altar, consider your intention for it. Will you use it for healing, remembering, protecting, manifesting, or all of these purposes? Your altar could be a place of personal integration, where you synthesize various aspects of your self and your life. Other altars might honor transitions, such as birth, marriage, relocation, or the seasons. Many ancient altars were places to give thanks and make offerings to the gods. Gratitude is a powerful and often neglected emotion, one that helps perpetuate reciprocity, so you might consider creating an altar dedicated to gratitude.

Visualize Your Altar

Try to visualize your altar in your mind's eye. The imagination is a powerful tool that can connect you with your unconscious; so open yourself up to whatever enters your mind. Are there colors, shapes, patterns, and specific objects that seem important? How do these elements relate to the purpose of your altar?

Locate Your Altar

Where will your altar be located—inside or outside? If it's inside, do you see an existing structure supporting it, such as a table, fireplace mantel, or bookshelf? Or is your altar's structure something new that you need to build or assemble? If your altar is outside, is it in a specific location, such as your garden, tucked into a hollowed-out tree, or atop an old bird bath? How does the location of the altar serve your intention for it?

An outdoor altar created with found objects

A musician's altar in a recording studio

Center, Purify, and Create

After you have gathered the sacred objects that you'll keep on your altar—and this might take hours or weeks—center yourself before putting the altar together. By centering, we mean quieting the everyday mind and entering a more peaceful, meditative state. You might want to first create sacred space by purifying the area where you will assemble your altar. Do this by burning incense or sage, which are both used ceremonially for purposes of purification. Once you have purified the space, you're ready to create your altar. Your altar, like your life,

An altar in a water garden at Ten Thousand Waves, Santa Fe, New Mexico

At the Threshold Between Heaven and Earth

will go through changes with the passage of time. Let your altar evolve by rearranging, adding, and removing objects when the spirit moves you.

Using Your Altar

Once you've created your altar, you might want to dedicate it. Your dedication ritual can be as simple as stating your intention for the altar or offering a prayer, or it could be an elaborate ritual. Once dedicated, your altar needs to be kept "alive"; that is, you need to sustain its connection to the sacred by using it regularly, whether that be once a day or once a week. If your altar includes candles, light them as part of a prayer or ritual on holidays, anniversaries, equinoxes, solstices, full moons, and other occasions that have meaning for you. You might burn incense on your altar, have a quiet cup of tea in front of it, or simply use it as a place to pray and meditate. If it feels appropriate, share your altar with others on occasion. Make it a place of celebration or prayer with family and friends. Finally, keep your altar clean. When you clean your altar, you pay attention to it and imbue it with your consciousness. The humble chore of cleaning can renew your connection with your altar.

An equestrian's personal altar

Any object, intensely regarded, may be a gate of access to the incorruptible eon of the gods.

—JAMES JOYCE

THIS IS A PLACE

where you can simply experience
and bring forth what you are and what you
might be. This is the place of creative
incubation. At first you might find that
nothing happens there.
But if you have a sacred place and use it,
something eventually will happen. . . .Your
sacred space is where
you find yourself again and again.

—*Joseph Campbell*

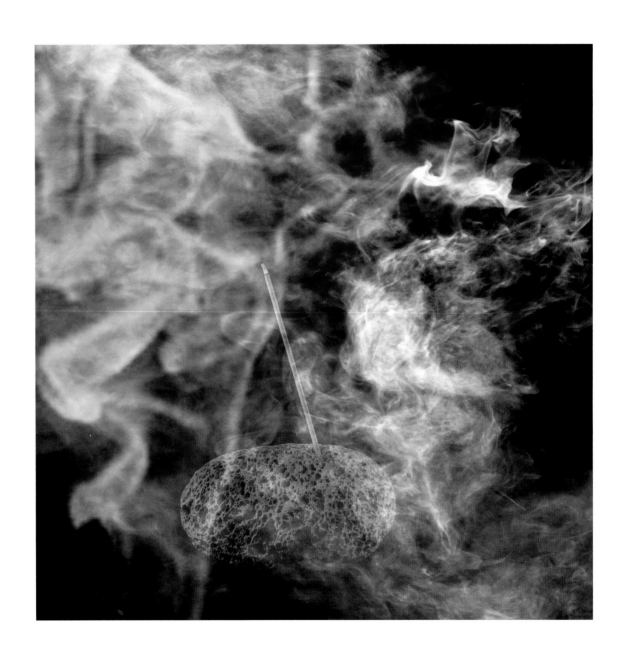

Sanctuary in Smoke
INCENSE AND SMUDGING

In an Anglican church, a priest swings a censer back and forth, releasing wisps of aromatic smoke that linger in the air like spirits. On the 27th night of Ramadan, the Islamic holy fast, a Muslim burns incense to dispel negative energy. Every morning and night, during the Hindu ceremony called *Agni Hota*, or Holy Fire, the devout light a ritual fire on which they burn incense. Participants in the Japanese *Kohdo* ritual, or "the way of incense," concentrate intensely in order to "listen" to the fragrances being burned. And prior to a sweat lodge ceremony, a Lakota smudges, or burns sage, to purify the participants and ceremonial space.

As part of their faiths, people from all over the world engage in the burning of aromatics, or incense, a practice that probably dates back to the discovery of fire. Plant resins (frankincense, myrrh, and copal), aromatic woods (sandalwood, agar wood, and cinnamon), and herbs (lavender, rosemary, and sage) were intentionally burned for the effects of their aromatic smoke. When our ancestors first observed that smoke rises, it came to symbolize the union of heaven and earth, and spirit and matter. As a result, smoke became a vehicle for communication with the spirit world, capable of carrying our prayers to heaven. For Buddhists, who use incense as an integral part of meditation, the rising smoke and fragrance of incense symbolizes unity with the higher realms of consciousness. Similarly, in the Christian tradition, incense smoke represents prayers ascending to heaven to honor God and the saints. Because Hindus view rising smoke as a way to carry the soul to the beyond, they use incense ceremonially during cremation to support the journey of the deceased to the afterlife.

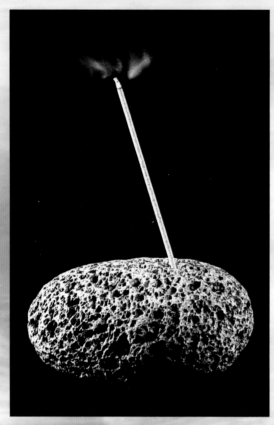

Many spiritual traditions hold that smoke can be a vehicle for communication with the spirit world.

Burning aromatics is also an ancient way of gaining access to the spirit of plants. Through thousands of years of exploring the mysteries of the botanical world, people came to know the characteristics of many plants, including those qualities released during burning. The word,

"perfume," which comes from the Latin, *par fumare*, means "through smoke," and many cultures have long believed that the wisdom and energy in a plant can be released by burning it. The spirit, or power, of a plant might heal the body, soothe the soul, facilitate communication with the gods, or impart wisdom to us about ourselves and the world.

One of the rituals involving the ceremonial burning of dried plants, called "smudging," comes from Native American traditions. These traditions teach that the smoke of burning plants, such as wild sage, sweetgrass, pine, and juniper, strengthens us, gives us courage, helps us on our spiritual journeys, and connects us to the sacred. During the ritual of smudging, a space, individual, or group is bathed in aromatic smoke, clearing the air, as well as the hearts and minds of those present.

I have often used incense to alter my own spiritual state, most often burning sage to change the energy in a situation or location. There is something about the aromatic smoke that, ironic as it sounds, always seems to clear the air. Occasionally, I have a night in which I just can't fall asleep. For what seems like an eternity, I toss and turn, unable to find comfort in any position. Eventually, insomnia drives me to a "dark night of the soul," an engagement with my shadow self in which I am barraged by every sadness, failure, and fear that I harbor. By day these feelings have little power over me; but during a sleepless night, they can gather over my bed like storm clouds. When this happens, I crave the scented smoke of white sage. I force myself out of bed, put a few dried leaves in an oyster shell, strike a match, and set the sage aflame. After a few seconds, I extinguish the tiny fire and fan its smoke around myself and the room. The familiar earthy aroma immediately calms me and soothes my spirit.

In recent times, the practice of smudging has been widely adopted by people of diverse cultural and spiritual backgrounds. Healers, in particular, are drawn to the power of smudging. Massage therapists, acupuncturists, and others use it to clear the energy in their offices between clients, and it is used in the reception areas of spas to prepare clients for the relaxing treatments that await them. Have you ever experienced a night that never seems to end? Now imagine the smoke from burning sage hanging in the air like the warm breath of the approaching sunrise, enveloping you in an aromatic sanctuary in which you discover the clarity of heart and soul that you need.

*Smells are surer
than sounds
and sights
to make
heartstrings crack.*
—RUDYARD KIPLING

Incense offering in a Thai temple

Making a Smudge Stick

Smudging can be performed by using a smudge stick—a bundle of dried herbs bound together with string—or by burning loose, dried leaves in a shell or other fireproof container.

Generally, sage is used for purifying, because Native Americans believe that it banishes negative energy, whereas sweetgrass, in contrast, calls forth good energy. You can make a smudge stick by using just one type of plant, such as sage, or, you can make a smudge stick by combining any of the following plants: sage, cedar, juniper, pinon pine, and rosemary (see page 37).

What You Need

Fresh plant sprigs (dried sprigs crumble too easily), cotton string or thread.

Arranging the Sprigs

Cut fresh sprigs about 4 to 6 inches in length. Select a sturdy and lengthy sprig as a base, and arrange other sprigs around it until you have a diameter of about an inch or so.

Wrapping the Bundle

Once you have the sprigs arranged, wrap the string around the bundle, starting at the bottom.

Figure 1

Figure 2

Use only cotton string or thread because synthetic fibers can produce noxious fumes. You need to wind the string around the base several times to secure it tightly (Figure 1). After the base is secure, wrap the string up and around the rest of the bundle several times (Figure 2). The string should be fairly tight as the plants will shrink as they dehydrate.

Drying the Smudge Stick

When you are finished wrapping your smudge stick, hang it in a cool dry place, out of direct sunlight, until the sprigs no longer feel moist.

To accelerate the drying process, you can wrap your smudge stick tightly in old newspapers or sheets of newsprint, changing the paper every few days until the smudge stick dries (usually within a week, depending upon humidity).

Smudging

To smudge, light the end of the smudge stick (or loose leaves in a bowl or shell), let the sprigs burn for a few seconds, and then gently blow on it to extinguish the flame. Fan the embers to keep them smoldering and producing smoke. When smudging a space, carry the smudge stick

The finished smudge stick

Sage and other aromatic herbs can also be burned "loose" in shells and other fire-proof containers.

or pot of smoking leaves around the space. When smudging yourself or another individual, the intent is not to inhale the smoke, but to allow it to wash over the person. Use a fan, feather, or your hands to circulate the smoke evenly around the person you are smudging, but try to keep a healthy "breathing space" at all times.

Smudge sticks can include decorative elements, such as dried flowers and colored thread, as long as the elements are non-toxic when burned, or are removed before burning.

PROPERTIES AND USES OF RESINS AND HERBS

A variety of resins, woods, barks, and other plant material is used in incense and smudging. Below is a list of some of the more popular plants used in aromatic burning and some of the healing properties and symbolism with which they are associated.

Resins

Frankincense: *communicating with a higher plane, healing, stress reduction*

Myrrh: *calming, well-being, grounding*

Benzoin: *imagination, creativity, inner peace*

Copal: *spiritual cleansing, grounding, inspiration, healing*

Wood and Bark

Sandalwood: *vitality, stress-relief, harmony*

Agars wood/Aloes wood: *centering, healing*

Cinnamon: *calming, sensuous, relaxing, opens the heart*

Plants and Herbs

Sage: *cleansing, healing, memory, wisdom, harmony*

Cedar: *energy, protection, luck, strength, decision making*

Sweetgrass: *cleansing, calls forth positive energy, healing*

Balsam: *happiness, luck, wealth, imagination*

Juniper: *cleansing, mental alertness, energy recharge*

Lavender: *clearing, cleansing, healing*

Rosemary: *mental strength, clarity, cleansing*

Pine: *protection, courage, emotional strength*

I DON'T FEEL LIKE WRITING A POEM,

Instead, I will light the incense-burning vessel

Filled with myrrh, jasmine, and frankincense,

And the poem will grow in my heart

Like flowers in my garden.

—*Student of Hafis*

Between Darkness and Light
THE ART OF CANDLE LIGHTING

One winter solstice, I gathered with a few friends to honor the year's longest night. Outside in the cold December night, we lit a candle and built a small fire for the new year. When the fire died down, we went into the house to enjoy dinner and exchange gifts. The next day I heard from my friend who had hosted the gathering. That morning, while walking her dog, she discovered that the candle was still burning. Apparently, when we left the cooling embers of the fire the night before, we had neglected to extinguish the candle and it had burned through the night. We were amazed that the candle had remained lit all night despite the winter winds and flurries. But more profound than its resistance to the elements was that the candle had burned throughout the longest and darkest night of the year, thereby symbolizing hope and promise for the year to come.

Most of the festivals that celebrate light occur during the height of celestial darkness. Advent, Chanukah, and Kwanza are all celebrated around the winter solstice, the longest night of the year. The celebration of Advent originated in the pre-Christian Germanic culture that sought the return of the sun at the darkest time of year by lighting candles arranged on an evergreen wreath. Christians adopted this ritual to celebrate the days leading up to Christmas. Chanukah, the Jewish festival of lights, celebrates the miracle of the temple lantern burning for eight days when it had only enough oil to burn for one. Kwanza, an African-American celebration, honors cultural unity, struggle, and the future, through the lighting of candles. And the Hindu festival of light, Deepawali, held on the darkest day of the new moon in late October or early November, celebrates the victory of goodness over evil and wisdom over ignorance. All of these festivals occur during the darkest time of year because it is then that we need light the most.

However, it's not just during the solstice that we express our reverence for light. All of the major world religions equate light with divinity. The Koran says, "Allah is the light of the heavens, and the earth"; the Hindus see Krishna as "the Lord of Light"; for Christians, Jesus is the "Light of the World"; and in Buddhist tradition, light is a reflection of truth. In many cosmologies, as well as in scientific theory, one of the first acts of creation is the emergence of light from darkness. In the Judeo-Christian Hexaemeron, on the first day of creation, God said, "Let there be light," and light was separated from darkness. However, the celestial bodies that we equate with naturally occurring light— the sun, moon, and stars—were not created until the fourth day. If the sources of light had

not yet been created, then from where did the light come? The origin of pre-celestial light has mystified clerics and scholars for centuries. Perhaps this primordial light symbolizes potential and the creative force, and every time we strike a flame, we symbolically touch that energy.

When we light a candle, we can call forth a power beyond our comprehension, one that asks the divine to see our light and carry us out of the darkness.

Light is unfathomable and wondrous—it is the stuff of creation, divinity, spirit, and hope. Light travels faster, longer, and farther than anything known. It's hard to believe that when we look at the stars, we are seeing ancient light that has traveled for millennia before finally reaching our eyes. The anomalous behavior of light, explored in the two most important scientific theories of the twentieth century—Einstein's relativity theory and quantum mechanics—continues to puzzle even the greatest minds in modern science. Einstein once said, "For the rest of my life I will reflect on what light is!" As for myself, I am grateful for the mystery of light, and I hope that it is never reduced to scientific formulae. But even if the mysteries of light eventually yield to science, our candles will continue to represent and invoke the pre-celestial light of creation that came out of the darkness.

The Art of Candle Lighting

Candles are one of the most ancient ways of providing light, so they have come to be the quintessential symbol of light, representing spiritual illumination and the aspiring human soul. Candles are used extensively in many spiritual traditions to sanctify space and enliven prayers. Lighting candles can reconnect you with the ancient and universal human yearning to create a light in the darkness. Candle lighting is therefore one of the oldest and most important rituals. It is also one of the simplest ways to ritualize an occasion and invite the sacred into the moment. For most of us, the first candle ritual in which we participated was making a wish while blowing out our birthday candles. This seemingly secular use of candles isn't very different from the many religious rituals in which a candle represents faith, hope, and spiritual light. There are many ways to use candles ritually. Here are a few suggestions.

To Create Sacred Space or Time

Lighting candles can sanctify almost any occasion. One occasion that always presents an opportunity to light candles is a meal. The Jewish Shabbat (Sabbath), a ritual that commemorates the period of time in which God rested after creation, is an example of a candle-lighting ritual that occurs around a meal. At the end of the work week, on Friday night, Jews light candles at sundown to mark the start of the Shabbat. They recite prayers of praise to God and often share special foods.

There are many reasons—both traditional and personal—to light candles to ritualize the sharing of food with family or friends. Candle lighting can help to create a feeling of sanctity during a heartfelt conversation, a romantic dinner, journal or letter writing, or when you take a ritual bath. In all of these instances, lighting a candle signals that you are setting an intention to invite the sacred into your activity.

For Prayer or Meditation

Candle lighting as part of prayer or meditation exists in nearly every faith. You may want to assign a prayer or intention to a candle and then light it while praying or stating your intention. If you have an altar, light a candle each morning while you say your prayers for the day, or in the evening to express gratitude. Light a candle during meditation to help keep your mind focused.

For a Candlelight Vigil

"Vigil" means wakefulness, or "to watch," and vigils were traditionally held on the eve of a sacred feast. The Easter Vigil, which represents the victory of light over darkness, culminates on the eve of Easter with the lighting of the Paschal Candle. Today, candlelight vigils are also held

*Use your own light
and return to the
source of light.
This is called
practicing eternity.*
—Lao-tzu

The Art of Candle Lighting 45

in response to events that require solemn attention. Vigils are appropriate for times of fear, when we most need to recover hope and strength. One way to begin a group vigil is to light a central candle and then have each person light a candle from the central one. Or, you can pass the flame, so that each person lights a candle from the candle of the person standing next to him or her. When lighting the candles, have each person say a prayer or make a statement related to the purpose of the vigil. To end the ceremony, either let the candles safely burn out or extinguish the flames with a meaningful gesture of your own design.

To Commemorate

Buddhists place thousands of small brass lamps around sacred sites to commemorate the Buddha's birthday; Jews light the candles on a menorah to commemorate the reclaiming and rededication of the Temple. You can commemorate anniversaries of births, deaths, weddings, and other occasions with ritualized candle lighting.

Candlelight vigil in Kathmandu

The Necessity of Darkness

Light and darkness are complementary: two parts of a whole, cyclical in nature, and meaningless without the contrast of the other. The Chinese *T'ai Chi*, or yin and yang, symbol is a perfect example of this concept, with its interlocking curves of light and dark. In most mystical traditions, darkness and light are equally necessary aspects of creation because darkness is associated with gestation, which precedes birth, and with death, which precedes resurrection.

Author and theologian Matthew Fox reminds us of the necessity of darkness in his writings on Creation Spirituality. In *Original Blessing*, he describes one path of the spiritual journey as the "via negativa," or "the way of negation." On this path, we let go of what we have created and what we seek and "befriend the darkness." When we are on the via negativa, we embrace what Buddhism calls the great "nothing," which is the heart of the universe. We yield to the darkness so that, when the time comes, we can once again see the light, but with a deeper understanding of ourselves.

It isn't easy for most of us to embrace the darkness. For the past three centuries—since the start of the "Enlightenment"—darkness has fallen out of favor, and has been equated with ignorance, despair, and evil, rather than mystery, potential, and renewal. Spiritually, we shy away from the dark and its silence, preferring the distractions of light and sound that the modern world offers us. And, technologically, we've practically rendered darkness extinct with electricity and the seemingly never-ending string of lights wrapped around the planet. We have become a species that is afraid of the dark. We are even afraid of our own shadows, as the saying goes. In Jungian psychology, the shadow represents the part of ourselves that we would rather not know. But even these shadowy parts of ourselves—cowardly or selfish though they may be—are a part of who we are and denying them prevents us from living up to our true potential.

So the next time you are feeling spiritually dark, remember that our hearts started beating in the darkness of the womb, seeds germinate in the darkness of the earth, and the earth rests in the darkness of winter so that spring can return. We all need fallow time. Darkness is a gift—it's a great open space in which anything can happen. Surrender to it and the light will return.

THERE IS A LIGHT THAT SHINES

beyond all things on earth,

Beyond us all, beyond the heavens,

Beyond the highest, the very highest heavens.

This is the Light that shines in our heart.

—*Upanishads*

In Rhythm With the Beat of the Universe
DRUMMING

Every so often my heart skips a beat, racing ahead of itself. This always gives me pause. After all, during that split second my heart actually falls out of sync with its own rhythms. It's a startling sensation that always calls my attention to the archetypal one-two beat that has kept time for me since before I was born. Although our lives are full of rhythms, there is none more important to us than the beating of our own hearts. But we usually don't pay much attention to our pulse, unless it falls out of sync. This is the nature of rhythm—when we're in sync with it, everything feels effortless; when we're not, it's as if our hearts skipped a beat.

The entire universe vibrates—every galaxy, star, planet, molecule, and atom—and everything has a rhythm. A rhythm is anything that repeats itself in time: the phases of the moon, an oak tree dropping acorns in autumn, the pounding surf, our heartbeat. During our lives, we are immersed in all of these rhythms, beginning with the rush of blood through our mother's body while we are still in her womb. From the first beat of our hearts to the last, our lives are defined by rhythm. We may, through the course of our days, walk to the beats of many different drums. But ultimately there is one rhythm that all of us share—the pulse of life.

Drumming is an ancient technology for keeping time with this pulse: It reminds us that we all come from the same primeval sound that burst forth out of the silent void—the first beat of the universe. Because the drum can evoke a beating heart, thunder, the flapping of wings, the pounding surf, and

Stacks of *puja*, or ritual drums in Tongsa Dzong, Bhutan

so many other sounds that create the symphony of life, it symbolizes the voice of creation. For the Lakota Indians, the drum represents the voice of Wakan-Tanka, the Great Spirit; within the Hindu tradition, the drum symbolizes the destructive-creative power of Shiva; for Buddhists, it is the hidden power of the cosmos and the voice of Buddha; and in many African cultures, the drum is a powerful symbol of the heart. As an expression of primal sound, the drum is also a catalyst that makes things happen, as in the expression, "to drum up."

Drums have been around for more than eight thousand years and drumming has been practiced by nearly every civilization. As an echo of the larger rhythms of life, drums have been used in many kinds of rituals: birth and funeral, renewal and harvest, work and play, war and peace. The sound of the drum has been used as an acoustic amulet, to ward off evil and calamity, and as a medium for communicating with nature and the spirit world. In the Japanese religion of Shintoism, drums are used to speak to the spirits of animals, water, and fire. The hypnotic rhythms created by West African drummers are believed to pull the spirits of ancestors into the bodies of dancers, and the Kaluli drummers of New Guinea hear the sounds of the drum as the voices of the dead communicating with the living.

Within shamanic traditions, the shaman's role is that of mediator between the ordinary world and the spirit world, and shamans have described their drums as horses, canoes, or other vehicles that carry them to other worlds. The ancient Samoyed used the same word for "bow" as for "drum" because they perceived the drum as a way to "shoot" the shaman into the sky, meaning into altered states of consciousness. Practitioners of most shamanic traditions believe that drumming creates a portal between worlds—through which they journey from one realm to another. For this reason, a shaman sometimes has an assistant who maintains the drumming while he or she enters a trance state. In this way, the assistant keeps the portal open so that the shaman can find his or her way back from the spirit world.

It is unlikely that we remember the first time we created a percussive sound. It was probably a form of body percussion, like clapping. We may have then progressed to tapping on a table with a spoon, which at some point led to the quintessential toddler "drum set"—a collection of pots and pans. We are drawn to rhythm because it makes us want to move and join in its vibration. The drum is often used to call soldiers into battle or dancers to the dance because the percussive and rhythmic sound travels through our bodies to our hearts in a visceral

Japanese drummers perform at a festival.

way, breaking down resistance from within. This is why a song with a good beat gets us tapping our feet unconsciously—we quite literally can't resist the beat, and our bodies give in to the rhythm.

When one rhythm pulls another into its beat, it is described as "entrainment." The theory of entrainment proposes that if two rhythms are very similar, with sources in close proximity, they will usually fall into synchrony with each other. It is easier for the two rhythms to pulse together than in opposition because of the mutual influence they have on one another. Entrainment can happen in music, dance, even life itself, as when our rhythms and those of the world around us fall into sync. When our tempo is in sync with another's, we fall into entrainment with him or her and it is easier to communicate. Some people have even described falling in love as a particularly profound kind of entrainment. Conversely, when we are out of sync—whether with family, friends, work, or the greater rhythm of our lives—it's as if our hearts are skipping beats and we've lost our rhythm.

Ritual drumming can help us stay in sync with our own biological and emotional rhythms, as well as with the rhythms of nature. Like other meditational practices, drumming can help us focus our attention. Just as shamans use drumming to journey to the spirit world, we can drum to travel out of our heads and into our hearts and bodies. From there, drumming can pull us into a centered state where we can find peace, serenity, and the sacred. When an infant cries, we sometimes respond by holding him or her against our chests. There, the baby can feel the familiar beating of our heart and is comforted. The drum can serve a similar purpose: It helps us feel the beat of our own hearts and, in doing so, it connects us to the rhythm of the universe.

Drumming on Both Sides of the Brain

Drumming can have profound physiological effects—it can increase heart rate and blood flow, like other aerobic activities, but it can also bring on an alpha state in our brains and induce other changes in the central nervous system. The alpha state, characterized by brain waves that occur fourteen to twenty-one cycles per second, is associated with relaxation, creative flow, and euphoria. Drumming has also been shown to play a role in hemispheric synchronization, in which the left (rational) and right (creative) sides of the brain work together. With hemispheric synchronization, we more easily enter a transcendent state, which is characterized by creative flow, openness, and heightened awareness.

The Sacred Art of Drumming

Anyone can drum, regardless of musical ability. When groups get together for ritual drumming, it's often called a drumming circle. Drumming circles are held for meditation, healing, celebration, or for the purpose of getting in rhythmic sync with one another and the world. Ritual drumming is a creative collaboration that is usually unrehearsed and unstructured. In a drumming circle, it's easy to lose yourself in the group rhythm and feel a sense of belonging to a pulse greater than your own.

Recently, drumming circles have sprung up nearly everywhere, attracting people from all walks of life. Drumming in groups has such widespread appeal because it enables us to achieve a sense of communal rhythm. Although you can join an already existing drumming circle, it's easy to facilitate your own. All you need is people, drums, and a space, indoors or out. You might schedule the drumming to fall on a full moon, equinox, solstice, holiday, or other special occasion.

What You Need

Ask people to bring their own drum, if they have one. If they don't have a drum, suggest they use a found object, such as a bucket, pail, empty coffee can, pot, pan, or a wooden box. Many objects can become percussive instruments just by tapping them with your hand or a wooden spoon. To create a softer sound, wrap a scrap of fabric around the spoon and secure it with string.

The Sacred Space of a Circle

Once your group is gathered, ask everyone to sit in a circle with their drum. The circle is a powerful symbolic element, without beginning or end. It's not mere coincidence that most drums are circular. Just look up at the sun or moon—both are circles—and you see one of the first and most ancient symbols of humanity. The circle represents eternity, totality, and the divine. Arranging the drummers in a circle helps to create ceremonial space and a sense of community.

The Intention

Is there a purpose or intention for the drumming? Do you just want to get in sync with each other and the sacred through the power of rhythm? Perhaps there's something the group wants to drum up, pray for, or celebrate.

The Rhythm

Get the drumming started by softly tapping your drum, in whatever rhythm comes to you. Then, speaking over your tapping, tell the group that there are no rules, and invite everyone to start playing. You'll feel a rhythm take form almost instantly, as if you could read each others' minds. As you continue drumming, allow people to improvise and let the rhythm change on a whim. Either take breaks together or allow individuals to break as they need to. You can let the drumming circle conclude spontaneously or you could suggest an intentional conclusion, such as a few minutes of drumming in a joyous tempo or a gradual slowing down into silence.

I CAN ONLY GAZE AT THE UNIVERSE

In its full, true form,

At the millions of stars in the sky

Carrying their huge harmonious beauty—

Never breaking their rhythm

Or losing their tune. . .

—*Rabindranath Tagore*

Returning to the Source
A RITUAL BATH

As I submerge myself in the bath, I try to imagine life without water, but it's impossible. Water is everywhere—from the soft, ghostly vapor of an early morning fog to the titanic swells of a tsunami. And wherever there's water, there's probably life. Millions of miles from Earth, satellites search for evidence of water on Mars, Venus, and Europa. We look for water on these celestial bodies because its presence suggests the possibility of life. But water doesn't merely offer the opportunity for life to arise; in many ways, water is life. On Earth, life is mostly liquid: our bodies are more than three-quarters water and we're not unique in these proportions. Because of water's ubiquity—both inside and outside the organisms it supports—scientists have mused that life may be just a way for water to get up and move around. As for myself, I believe that the watery nature of life keeps all of creation connected to its origins.

We know that life began in the primordial seas that covered most of the Earth following its formation, and for us, life still begins in water—in the aquatic cradle of the womb. Therefore, water embodies the idea of creative potential. The Koran states that "We have created every living thing from water," and in the Bible, God's Spirit stirred upon the surface of the waters. The magical alchemy that brought forth life from water may be the reason that water can have such a renewing effect on our physical, emotional, and spiritual well-being. When I'm going through a difficult time, I am often called to water. In the warm womblike waters of the bath, I reconnect with my own potential for change, and my perspective shifts from fixed to fluid. Troubles seem to wash away and I emerge renewed. But water's rejuvenating effects are not limited to the bath. Nature's waters can be particularly transformative. When I swim in a river, I feel the current of my life and yield to it, trusting that the waters will flow where they are meant to. In the sea, I am reminded of my own salty origins—of the brackish blood, sweat, and tears that flow through my body, driven by the rhythm of my heart. I feel the lunar pull on the water, and as the undertow calls me back to that saline source of life, my pulse entrains with the rising and subsiding tide, and I feel reconnected to the mother element.

It's no wonder that so many cultures have rituals of renewal that involve immersion in water. When we immerse ourselves in water, it's difficult not to feel its influence on our bodies and souls. Consequently, water is considered sacred by many spiritual traditions. The renewing and purifying properties of water gave rise to the ritual of baptism, in which the participant is purified, renewed, or "born again" through initiation. In ancient Greece, baptism was associated with the worship of goddesses who emerged from water. According to myth, Aphrodite, the Greek goddess of love, rose out of the sea foam

Baptismal font
(Saint Andrew's
Episcopal Church,
Marblehead,
Massachusetts)

on a scallop shell. Upon emerging from the ocean, she immersed herself in a sacred bath that restored her virginity. This bath became a ritual that was re-enacted every spring by the high priestess of Aphrodite's temple. Goddesses from other myths and traditions were also said to take virginity-restoring ritual baths. The restoration was symbolic, implying not an absence of sexuality, but rather a sense of renewal and hope.

Ritual purification with water still exists today. Tibetan monks prepare for devotion with a ritual cleansing of the mouth. Outside of Shinto shrines and tea houses in Japan, there are stone water troughs and dippers, which are used to clean fingers and mouths before entering. The Ganges river, sacred within the Indian tradition, is believed to purify those who ritually immerse themselves in it. Hindus believe that the waters of the Ganges can break the cycle of re-incarnation, which,

Immersing one's self in a "cold plunge" after soaking in hot water can reawaken the senses. (Ten Thousand Waves, Santa Fe, New Mexico.)

*If there is magic
on this planet,
it is contained
in water.*

— LOREN EISELEY

In traditional Japanese bathing a wooden bucket is used for washing and rinsing before getting into the tub. (Ten Thousand Waves, Santa Fe, New Mexico.)

in the Hindu tradition, is the ultimate spiritual goal. Zen monks sometimes sit under an icy waterfall to wash away attachment, and Cherokees immerse themselves in a stream to dissolve the veil that separates them from their visions. In Islam, a ritual ablution every morning restores a Muslim to purity before facing Allah; Orthodox Jews perform a ritual morning washing; and Christians baptize an initiate to signify rebirth in Christ.

Within the psychoanalytic tradition, which draws upon symbolism, mythology, and ritual, water is a symbol of the unconscious. It represents that mysterious part of our psyche that manifests in prayer, meditation, dreams, and the imagination. Symbolically, when we immerse ourselves in water, we bring the ego—the part of our psyche that governs our waking consciousness—into contact with the unconscious, or submerged parts of ourselves. In Taoism, the state of potentiality associated with the unconscious is called the "tao," and to return to this state is to return to the source. When we immerse ourselves in water, we break through the illusive barrier, and, like the Cherokee who sits in a stream to dissolve the veil that separates him from his visions, we return to a place where all things are again possible.

Taking a Ritual Bath

The world is the river of God, flowing from him and flowing back to him.

—UPANISHADS

The bath has been considered a sublime method of relaxation since the beginning of recorded history. But the bath can go beyond relaxation, for taken with intention, it can become a personal ritual of renewal.

Create Sacred Space
You can begin your ritual bath by lighting candles, burning incense, and/or playing relaxing music. Make yourself as comfortable as possible by ensuring that the room is an appropriate temperature and by eliminating any potential distractions, such as a ringing telephone.

Set Your Intention
What is your intention for your ritual bath? Do you want the bath to help you let go of specific feelings or do you simply want to feel renewed?

Immerse Yourself in the Experience
As you settle into the bath, let go of everyday thoughts, concerns, and problems, and connect with your senses. Feel the water engulf you. Smell any fragrance you may have added. Listen to the way the water sounds as you gently wash it over yourself. Sometimes, you need to lose yourself before you can find yourself, so let go of your ego by slipping under the surface for a few seconds or by splashing your face. Let yourself merge with the bath as if you were a river and it the sea.

Invite nature into your bath by floating flower blossoms in the water. (Ten Thousand Waves, Santa Fe, New Mexico.)

An Aromatic Bath

You can further enrich the bathing ritual by taking an aromatic bath. Aromatherapy is the ancient art and science of caring for body and mind through the application of essential oils derived from grasses, herbs, flowers, and trees. Since antiquity, priests, alchemists, and healers have used plants for their medicinal and mystical properties. Essential oils affect our physical and psychological selves, exerting subtle influences on our bodies, emotions, and moods. Wafting upwards from the warm bathwater to our noses and absorbing gently through our skin, the natural compounds released from a few drops of pure essential oil gently restore our spirit and revitalize our body, enhancing the benefits of the bath.

To create an aromatic bath, use four to six drops of a single essential oil or a combination of oils per bath. Important: If you are pregnant or have allergies, check with your doctor before using essential oils.

Qualities of Essential Oils

Bergamot	*uplifting*
Chamomile	*soothing*
Cedarwood	*harmonizing*
Clary Sage	*relaxing*
Cinnamon	*warming*
Eucalyptus	*stimulating*
Ginger	*stimulating*
Juniper	*regenerating*
Lavender	*balancing*
Lemon	*refreshing*
Orange	*stimulating*
Neroli	*calming*
Pine	*cleansing*
Rosemary	*invigorating*
Rose	*calming*
Sage	*clarifying*
Tea Tree	*cooling*

ITS SUBSTANCE REACHES EVERYWHERE;

it touches the past and

prepares the future;

it moves under the poles

and wanders thinly in the heights of air.

It can assume forms of

exquisite perfection in a snowflake,

or strip the living to a single shining bone

cast up by the sea.

—*Loren Eiseley*

PART TWO

Ways
to the Center

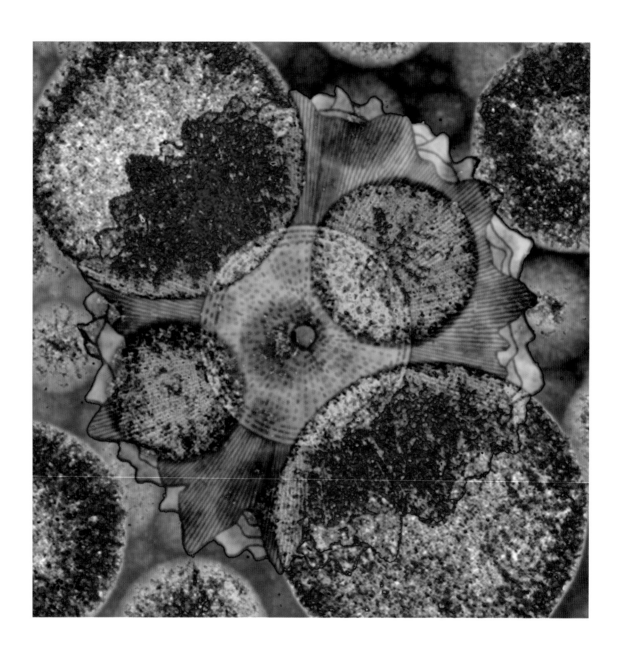

Finding One's Center
MEDITATING WITH MANDALAS

When I am centered, I feel connected to the very core of my being, where almost anything seems possible. I can more easily overcome my perceived limitations and better access my strengths. Sometimes I can merge with an activity in a state of flow; other times I discover an inner silence that awakens me to the sacred. But finding my center isn't easy. Life all too often has me running in circles around myself, rather than centering within myself. At those chaotic times, I try to remember that all circles have a center from which the concentric energies radiate. Then I try to find that quiet place of potential in myself by moving through my thoughts, feelings, and actions until I arrive at the calm eye of the storm: my center.

Within many spiritual traditions, "centering" is an important part of meditation, contemplative prayer, and sacred ceremony. Different faiths have created a variety of ritual tools that help facilitate centering, such as mantras, prayers, ritualized gestures, and mandalas. Mandalas are ancient and nearly universal forms of sacred geometric art, usually comprised of concentric shapes and symbolic images. They are used for many different types of spiritual practices, such as meditation, healing, initiation, teaching, and prayer. Mandalas appear in the complex patterns of Islamic art, in the knotwork of the ancient Celts, in the sand paintings of the Tibetan and Navajo (Diné) peoples, and in the sacred art of Christian mystics, like Hildegard of Bingen and Jacob Boehme. Mandalas are sometimes described as cosmograms, or maps of the cosmos, because they can express a divine hierarchy. For example, the well-known rose window mandala in the Notre Dame Cathedral depicts kings and high priests in the outer circle; judges in the central circle; prophets of the Old Testament in the inner circle, and the Virgin Mary with the infant Jesus in the center.

Mandala is the Sanskrit word for "circle"—or center and circumference—and the essential meaning of the mandala derives from the symbolism of these two aspects of the circle. The circumference—what we usually call a circle—is a form without a beginning or an end. It is one of the most important and universal symbols in human history, representing wholeness, completeness, and the cyclical nature of life.

The circle contains all the parts of the whole, but is more than the sum of its parts because it includes the center—a powerful and sacred symbol that represents potential and the movement outward of the one toward the many. The center represents the seed from which the tree grows, the cell that divides to make the seed, the atoms that make up the cells, the nucleus that lies at the heart of the atom, and so on, ad infinitum. The two aspects of the circle—the potential of its center and the totality of its circumference—are embodied in the mandala's strong central focal point and surrounding concentric forms. In Tibetan Buddhism, mandalas are the symbolic terrain of the soul's journey to enlightenment. The design of the mandala guides the meditator toward its center. Radiating out from the center, in concentric layers, are geometric shapes and ancient spiritual icons that symbolize different phases of initiation or levels of consciousness. Every element of the mandala—shape, color, pattern, and imagery—represents a principle or aspect of wisdom related to the lesson it teaches.

Within the Hindu tradition, the mandala takes the form of the *yantra*, a sacred diagram intended to guide the meditator to experience unity with the center, known as the bindu, or absolute. The center of a yantra is the undifferentiated infinite, from which all matter and spirit emanate. It is the originating point of divine consciousness, and the cosmic unity that underlies the multiplicity of the world. Everything issues from and returns to this point, expanding in concentric forms. One of the Hindu sacred texts, the Upanishads, uses the metaphor of a spider at the center of its simultaneously expanding and contracting web to illustrate the

Everything
the Power of the World does is
done in a circle. The sky is round, and I
have heard that the earth is round like a ball,
and so are all the stars. The wind, in its greatest
power, whirls. Birds make their nests in circles, for
theirs is the same religion as ours. The sun comes forth
and goes down again in a circle. The moon does the
same, and both are round. Even the seasons form a
great circle in their changing, and always come back
again to where they were. The life of a man is a
circle from childhood to childhood, and so it
is in everything where power moves.

—*Black Elk*

concept of the center and its relationship to the forms it manifests. Just as all of existence originates from a central point, every individual has his or her own inner center.

The widespread cross-cultural use of the mandala inspired psychoanalyst Carl Jung to recognize it as an archetype—a psychological pattern that shapes the human psyche. Jung's research demonstrated that the mandala isn't a form we create so much as an energy we express. The urge to create and gaze upon a mandala is a universal tendency of human consciousness just as nest-building is inherent in the consciousness of most birds. Jung saw the mandala as an expression of the human longing to be psychologically and spiritually integrated. He believed that the symbolic expression of wholeness manifested by the mandala could help people connect with their deeper selves, so he used it as a therapeutic tool, encouraging his patients to create mandalas in their quest to achieve their full potential.

Just as the power of the world often manifests in circles, our own power, or potential, can also be discovered in a circle. The mandala can take us to the still point in ourselves, where we can reconnect with the sacred by encountering the possibilities that emanate from the center.

The nature of God
is a circle
in which the center
is everywhere
and the circumference
is nowhere.
        —EMPEDOCLES

Mandala painting, Tongsa Dzong, Bhutan

Meditating with Mandalas 77

Yantras are Hindu mandalas used as meditation tools. The *Sri Yantra,* depicted here, is considered the most auspicious of all yantras, as it represents the totality of existence. Using the Sri Yantra in meditation is said to help the meditator realize his or her unity with the absolute, thereby bringing peace and happiness.

Nature's Mandalas

Nature is filled with mandalas. On the micro-cosmic level, flowers, eggs, seeds, spider webs, cross-sections of plant stems and tree trunks, snowflakes, mineral crystals, cells, molecules, and atoms are mandalas; on the macro-cosmic level, planets and their orbits, solar systems and galaxies are mandalas. The human eye also has a mandalic form: The pupil sits in the center of the iris, collecting light from the outer world and pro-jecting it inward. Even the paracrystalline form of the DNA molecule is a mandala, and when photographed from a particular angle, it's even a square within a circle, like many Tibetan mandalas!

Create a Meditation Mandala

The mandala is a visual journey through layers of consciousness to the center, where we can experience our own potential as well as the sacred. You can take this journey by creating a mandala as well as by using one as a meditation tool. After creating your mandala, explore the symbolic meaning of its elements by reading the Mandala Symbolism Chart on page 83.

Artistic ability has nothing to do with making a mandala. Making a mandala is an expression of the patterns and flow of energy emanating from you at the time you create it. This energy manifests in color, form, and number, as well as personal and archetypal imagery.

Don't judge your mandala the way you might critique an exercise in a drawing class! If you are creating individual mandalas in a group setting, arrange the space so that everyone has a private work area and separate materials. After you've created your mandala, you can share it with others, but while you are making it, it's best to resist looking at the mandalas others are making.

What You Need

You'll need paper and paint, colored pencils, markers, or pastels, depending upon which medium you choose. You can also use drawing tools, such as a protractor or French curve, but

Spontaneously created mandalas, such as these, are visual representations of the mandala makers' psychic energies.

try not to let these tools limit the form of your mandala. If you want to create an assemblage, or collage mandala from three-dimensional objects, such as stones, shells, beads, or other items that you can collect in substantial quantities, adapt these instructions as necessary.

Center and Visualize

Close your eyes and try to enter a peaceful, meditative state. Take deep breaths and with each exhalation release any expectations of what you think your mandala should look like. Now, allow a circle to emerge from your imaginative vision. Without judgment, allow feelings, shapes, colors, and patterns to come to you. Sit

with these images for a few minutes and allow, but don't force, them to change. Let them fill the circle in whatever way they want to, forming the mandala. When the mandala image feels complete, you are ready to begin drawing.

Create the Mandala

Open your eyes, select a color, and draw a circle by using a compass or by tracing a circular object, such as a plate. Starting at the center, fill the circle with colors, forms, and images, allowing the mandala to continue to change while you are drawing it (you do not need to be faithful to the mandala that you visualized when your eyes were closed). Try not to think too

much about what you're doing, for you are really allowing the mandala to create itself.

Explore the Mandala's Symbolism

When the mandala is complete, use the Mandala Symbolism Chart to learn the basic meaning of colors, shapes, and numbers. Note that "number" is reflected in your mandala as the frequency with which a particular form occurs. For example, if you have eight points radiating from a shape, you would look at the symbolism for the number eight. Keep in mind that all three of the mandala components listed on the chart should be considered together, not in isolation. For example, if you have eight green

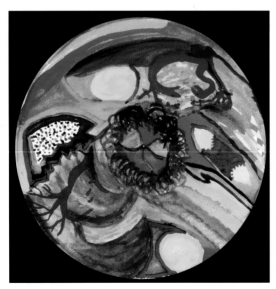

triangular points, you would look at the symbolism of the number eight, the color green, and the triangle. Consider the symbolism holistically, within both the larger context of the entire mandala and of your past and present life. Also consider your personal associations with colors, shapes, numbers, and other imagery.

Meditate with Your Mandala

Once you've created your mandala, you can use it as a meditation tool to center and strengthen awareness. Begin by looking at the mandala from different orientations in order to find out which one feels right. Then position the mandala at eye level by tacking it on a wall or resting it on a piece of furniture. Sit in a comfortable position, quiet yourself, then focus on the mandala. Try to keep your gaze soft, but steady. Only the mandala should occupy your mind; try not to let your concentration drift. Once you've acquired a strong image of the mandala, close your eyes, letting the image fill your consciousness. If the image fades, open your eyes and concentrate on the mandala again. Continue in this way until you feel your mind is still. If you practice this meditation over time, you may find that it centers you and strengthens your awareness.

MANDALA SYMBOLISM CHART

Creating a mandala can reveal the invisible forms of the unconscious by presenting them in symbolic images that we can comprehend. These symbols can connect us to hidden parts of ourselves, thereby making us more complete. Use this chart to explore some of the symbolism that might be embodied in your mandala.

COLOR

Red life, energy, impulse, aggression, joy

Blue divinity, truth, faith, loyalty, peace

Yellow warmth, clarity, consciousness, comprehension

Green fertility, spring, youth, renewal, paradise, envy

Orange willfulness, drive, happiness, warmth

Purple magic, royalty, dignity, spirituality, imagination, vanity

White light, creation, spirit, purity, truth, initiation, peace

Black mystery, darkness, despair, evil, gestation, germination

SHAPE

Circle completion, wholeness, cycles, protection, cosmos, sacred space

Cross conjunction, intersection, energy, fire

Spiral evolution, involution, order, change, flow

Square permanence, proportion, equity, balance, materiality, earth

Star guidance, aspiration, destiny, hope, constancy

Triangle light, fire, harmony, ascension

NUMBER

One creation, origin, totality, center, God, individual

Two multiplicity, separation, symmetry, equilibrium

Three creativity, synthesis, reunion, unity, harmony, luck, magic

Four solidity, stability, justice, power, balance, materiality, earth

Five totality, meditation, analysis, integration, love

Six union, equilibrium, completion, chance

Seven magic, mysticism, orientation, spiritual order, protection, perfection

Eight cosmic equilibrium, renewal, stability, totality

Nine truth, order, endurance, synthesis

Ten totality, perfection, reality, action

Eleven transition, conflict, excess, danger, discord, rebirth

Twelve cosmic order, celestial influence, cycles, salvation, union of spiritual and material

SELF IS EVERYWHERE,

shining forth from all beings, vaster than
the vast, subtler than the most subtle, unreachable,
yet nearer than breath, than heartbeat. Eye cannot
see it, ear cannot hear it, nor tongue utter it; only
in deep absorption can the mind, grown pure and
silent, merge with the formless truth.
As soon as you have found it, you are free,
you have found yourself; you have solved the great
riddle; your heart is forever at peace.
Whole, you enter the Whole.

—Upanishads

The Greatness of Little Things
THE WAY OF TEA

To get to the teahouse, I walked through a small Japanese garden on a path of stepping stones. I stopped to wash my hands at a bamboo fountain that tumbled water into a rock basin. Just outside the teahouse, I removed my shoes and then silently entered through a small door, on my knees. The teahouse floor was spread with *tatami* mats and the light was pleasantly subdued. My host, Mr. Aso, awaited me inside, also on his knees. After all the guests had entered, we bowed in greeting and then, staying on our knees at all times, took the place appointed to us by the tea apprentice. A painting of an apple—a symbolic honoring of the onset of autumn—was hung in the *tokonoma*—an alcove dedicated to the display of art.

The preparation of the tea began in silence. Time slows down during a tea ceremony, and nothing seems to exist except each moment. My senses seemed sharper than usual, and I noticed the most minute sounds, scents, and motions of the tea preparation. Watching the skilled movements of Mr. Aso's hands, it became apparent that every aspect of tea was truly art. The way he held, dipped, and released the bamboo dipper, the folding and unfolding of the cloth napkin, the sharp tap of the scoop against the tea bowl—all of these movements were part of a graceful choreography that held my attention and kept me centered in the moment. Although the bowl of tea that awaited us was an important part of the ceremony, its preparation was equally significant. One of the lessons that tea teaches us is that a mundane task, such as the making of tea, can become an expression of beauty.

In my hands I hold a bowl of tea. I see all of nature represented in its green color. Closing my eyes I find green mountains and pure water within my own heart. I feel these become part of me.

—ANONYMOUS

(Kaji Aso Studio and Institute for the Arts, Boston, Massachusetts.)

Just prior to serving the tea, Mr. Aso served us small Japanese pastries, providing a lingering taste of sweetness that would soon be balanced by the tea, which is slightly bitter. Most full-length tea ceremonies include the serving of a thin tea, followed by a thick tea. Our host began the thin tea preparation by pouring a dipperful of water into the tea bowl, vigorously stirring it with a bamboo whisk, and emptying the water into a jar. He wiped the tea bowl clean with the carefully folded cloth napkin and opened the pot of tea. Using a small bamboo scoop, he placed the powdered green leaf into the bowl and then added water from the stove using the bamboo dipper. He whipped the mixture into a frothy broth—often described as the color of liquid jade—with a small bamboo whisk the size of a shaving brush. The bowl was then passed to the first guest, who lingered over it for a moment, took several sips, wiped it clean with her napkin, and passed it to the next guest. In this way a single bowl of tea was shared by all three guests. After a bit of restful conversation, the thick tea was served.

Our host used an ancient coal stove to heat the water. The faint hissing and whistling of the stove suggested sounds of nature—a distant rainfall or a light wind rustling through leafy branches. At one point, I told Mr. Aso that I enjoyed the sounds created by the stove, and he

Here, *wa*, or harmony, is expressed by the presence of a single flower that quietly invites our appreciation of its beauty. (Kaji Aso Studio and Institute of the Arts, Boston, Massachusetts.)

The antique stove contributed to the *wa* of the tea experience, by creating a soft whistling sound reminiscent of the wind rustling through leafy branches. (Kaji Aso Studio and Institute of the Arts, Boston, Massachusetts)

warmly responded by saying how glad he was that I liked it. This simple but heartfelt exchange inspired a feeling of friendship despite the fact that I had known Mr. Aso for only an hour or two. It was then that I recalled a piece of calligraphy hanging at the entrance of the teahouse. It translated as "One moment full of friendship." This is part of what the tea ceremony is all about—the greatness of little things and the sacredness of simple acts. In that brief exchange, we were both fully present in the moment, in the enjoyment of the whistling kettle. That presence doesn't happen often enough in daily life.

Buddhist monks introduced the ritualized drinking of tea to Japan, often using tea as an antidote to drowsiness during meditation. Bodhidharma, the founder of Zen Buddhism, is credited with establishing the drinking of tea as a tradition. Later, Zen monks would drink tea out of a bowl while sitting before the image of Bodhidharma. This is thought by many scholars to be the origin of the tea ceremony. The altars in Zen monasteries—upon which flowers are offered and incense is burned—evolved into the *tokonoma*, the alcove in a tea room where art

Jaku, or *tranquility*, is an important part of the Japanese tea ceremony.

and flowers are displayed for the pleasure of the guests. The tea ceremony expresses many aspects of Zen Buddhism, as embodied in the Japanese saying, *chazen ichimi*, or "Zen and tea are one."

There is also a strong link between Taoism and tea. Tao means "path" or "way." In Japan, "ways" are the means by which tradition, art, and wisdom are learned and transmitted. *Chado*, the way of tea, manifests through *Chanoyu*, the Japanese tea ceremony. The way of tea embodies four principles: *wa* (harmony), *kei* (respect), *sei* (purity), and *jaku* (tranquility). *Wa* exists through the graceful blending of art forms, such as painting, flowers, incense, and tea, as well as through the harmonious engagement of all our senses. *Kei* is expressed in the bowing of guests and hosts, through the careful and reverent handling of the utensils, and through the ceremony itself, which honors nature, art, and tradition. *Sei* begins with the ritual purification at the fountain and continues through the public cleansing of the bowl before the making of the tea and the wiping of the bowl before it is

Hospitality
is
one
form
of
worship.
—The Talmud

The Way of Tea 91

*We work with
the stuff of the soul
by means of
the things of life.*
—THOMAS MOORE

passed to the next guest. Sei also manifests through purity of mind, which is achieved by guests quieting themselves internally. This way they can be present to what is happening in the moment—the taste, aroma, and appearance of the tea; the sweetness of the pastries; the art displayed in the tokonoma; and other aspects of the ceremony. Sometimes, Zen philosophy is included in the conversation, but rarely is the outside world mentioned, keeping the hearts and minds of host and guests pure. Finally, *jaku* manifests through the various silences, the leisurely pace of the ceremony, and the gentle demeanor of the host and guests.

Nearly every gesture in the tea ceremony has meaning. Walking through a garden before entering the teahouse allows guests to collect their

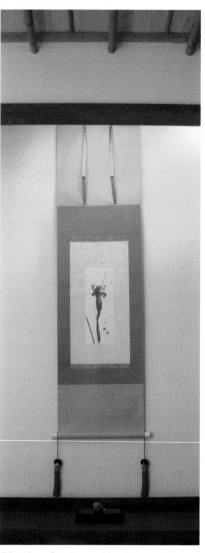

(Kaji Aso Studio and Institute of the Arts, Boston, Massachusetts)

thoughts and center themselves in the moment. The washing of hands at the fountain is a purification ritual in which one washes away the outside world. Bending and entering the teahouse on one's knees, as well as the subsequent kneeling and bowing, creates an atmosphere of humility. The tokonoma, with its display of paintings, calligraphy, and flowers, reminds one to appreciate beauty. But, more than anything else, the tea ceremony helps to sanctify the moment by inspiring us to be present in it. Many faiths tell us that every moment can be a source of grace and an opportunity to connect with the sacred. Tea reminds us that the sacred is always present—in a steaming bowl of liquid jade, in the admiration of a painting, in a moment full of friendship.

The Legendary Origins of Tea

According to legend, nearly 5,000 years ago in China, a sci-entifically-inclined emperor named Shen Nung declared that all drinking water should be boiled to ensure that it was safe to drink. One day, while traveling, the emperor stopped to rest, and his servants made a fire with which to boil water so that everyone could enjoy a drink. However, leaves from a nearby bush fell into the boiling water, changing its color. The emperor, having an inquisitive mind, tasted the water and found it appealing. He supposedly wrote in his diary that this new beverage quenched thirst, lessened the desire to sleep, and gladdened the heart. To this tale the Japanese add that the bush that shed its leaves into Shen Nung's water was planted by none other than the Buddhist monk Bodhi-dharma, who has since been credited with establishing the drinking of tea as a tradition.

Ways to Invite the Sacred to the Table

The tea ceremony takes years of practice to learn and even longer to master, and teaching it is not within the scope of this book. Nonetheless, it can serve as an example of how we can invite the sacred to the table.

When setting out to create a ceremony around food and drink, think about what you can bring to it. You can inform and shape your ceremony with your cultural and religious background, as well as your interest in and appreciation of other cultures, art, and even nature. Whether you implement only a simple act, such as having a moment of silence or sharing a blessing before a meal, or choreograph a ritualized harvest feast on the night of an autumnal full moon, consider the lessons of tea as you think about your ceremony. Be present in the moment, concentrate fully on what you are doing, and cultivate an awareness of beauty. View each and every task—from folding napkins to selecting the vegetables—with "tea mind," that unique quality of awareness that is infused with harmony, respect, purity, and tranquility. Tea Masters teach that when you fold a cloth napkin, you are folding the universe. So, approach every aspect of your ceremony as if you might experience the world in it. You will discover that there can be a profound peace in simplicity. Tea mind tells us that there is a greatness in little things. Believe it.

Here are suggestions for how you might use the four principles of tea to create sacred space for your ceremony or special occasion.

Harmony, or *Wa*

Try to engage all the senses in your ceremony. Bring your visual artistry to the table: Arrange flowers, fruit, branches, or other items to make a centerpiece, fold origami cranes as place tags, or create another type of artwork for the occasion. Burn incense, scented candles, or simmer potpourri to fill your space with fragrance. Select appropriate music to be played during your gathering, or arrange for a guest to perform before or after the food is served. When planning your menu, carefully consider how the various foods you serve will complement and enhance one another. Consider serving fresh seasonal foods as a way to celebrate nature's rhythms.

Respect, or *Kei*

Honor your guests, yourself, and the occasion with reverence. Treat each and every aspect of the ceremony as important. In this way you will help yourself and your guests to recognize the sacredness of simple acts. For example, send creative invitations, greet your guests formally when they arrive, deliver a toast that honors them, or send them home with a small homemade gift.

Purity, or *Sei*

Remember the saying: "Cleanliness is next to godliness," and make sure the place where you have your ceremony is clean and uncluttered. Consider the principle of purity from intellectual and spiritual perspectives as well. Try to clear your mind and heart of distracting thoughts and emotions so that you can be fully focused and present.

Tranquility, or *Jaku*

If possible, try to maintain a relaxed atmosphere by having most of the meal prepared in advance. In this way you will be able to spend more time with your guests and less in the role of a frenzied host or hostess. Play music that soothes the soul and use lighting that is easy on the eyes. Don't rush through anything; let the ceremony unfold gracefully, at its own pace.

How, but in custom and ceremony,
Are innocence and beauty born?

—W.B. YEATS

Simple, yet beautiful, utensils create a sense of elegance. (Kaji Aso Studio and Institute of the Arts, Boston, Massachusetts)

WHAT, THEN, DID THE TEA MASTERS SEE—
what did their vision disclose?
It was the reflection of the inner nature of
things, the reality of things, which the old
philosophers called "the eternal mode."
They saw the thing itself, the whole which is
entirely different from the sum of its parts.

—*Soetsu Yanagi*

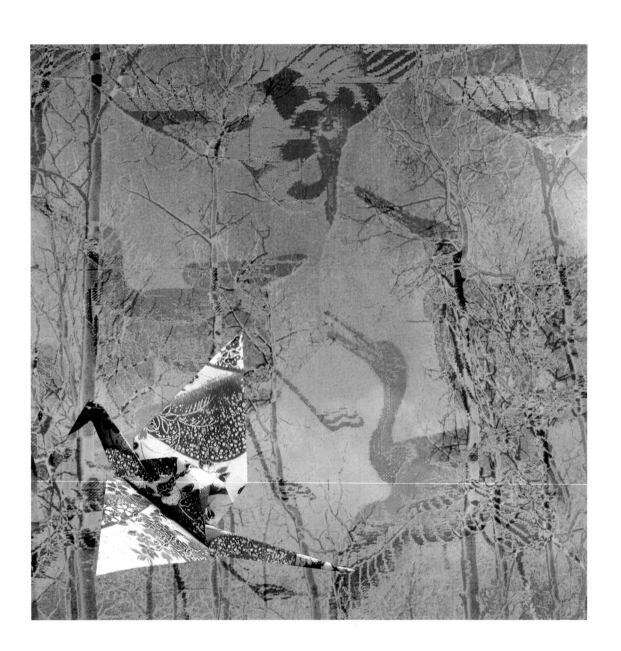

Unfolding Mindfulness
FOLDING ONE THOUSAND CRANES

Japanese legend holds that if you fold one thousand origami cranes, your wish will come true. Although the origin of the legend is a mystery, it relates to the symbolism of the crane, which, like many birds, has often been portrayed as a divine messenger. The crane's magnificent and powerful wings seem to enable it to touch the farthest reaches of the sky. In Japan, a legend from the eleventh century tells the story of a feudal leader who attached a strip of paper on which he'd written a prayer to the leg of a crane. He did this for each soldier killed in battle, and then freed the cranes to carry the prayers to the heavens. Cranes were also symbols of longevity and were credited with immensely long lifespans, as reflected in the folk saying, "Cranes live for one thousand years; turtles live for ten thousand years." The crane's one-thousand-year imaginary lifespan is reflected in the number of paper cranes you need to fold in order to have your wish fulfilled.

I first became interested in origami after seeing an exhibit and demonstration at a local museum. Shortly thereafter, I began teaching myself to fold various forms to entertain my then three-year-old daughter, and I was immediately drawn into the art of paper folding. I also became interested in the history of origami. It began in China around the first century C.E., and was brought to Japan by Buddhist monks in the early seventh century. In Japan, paper folding was originally used ceremonially, particularly in Shinto and Buddhist rites. In fact, the Japanese word for "paper," *kami*, is a homonym for the Shinto word for "spirit," and another translation of origami is "paper of the spirit." In traditional origami, the paper is never cut while making a form. This practice probably arose from the Shintoist respect for the plant spirit that gave its life so the paper could be made. In Shintoism, paper

*The beauty of
the Way
is that there is
no Way.*
— Loy Ching-Yuen

Cranes were symbols of longevity, as reflected in the folk saying, "Cranes live for one thousand years; turtles live for ten thousand years."

folded to symbolically represent the spirits has traditionally been hung in shrines to mark the boundary between the sacred and the profane. Another early Shinto ritual involved the whispering of prayers into pieces of paper that were then tied to trees. The Shintoists believed that every time the wind rustled the papers, the prayers were repeated.

After learning about the legend of folding one thousand cranes (known as *Senbazuru* in Japanese), I decided that I wanted to undertake the task. I made my wish and hoped the paper birds I was about to create would live up to their legendary potential and make my wish come true. I then selected exquisite Japanese papers that rendered tiny cranes with mere two-inch wingspans. As I began, I carefully chose the paper for each crane as if it were the only one I was making. I folded and admired each lovely bird as it shape-shifted from a flat sheet of paper into a graceful winged creature. I noticed the variations of the angles, the grain of the paper, and the subtle differences between the cranes. Every time I sat down to fold, I felt peaceful and centered, as if nothing else in the universe mattered except me and my paper birds.

But then, when I had folded about forty paper cranes, I began to plan what I would do with my delicate creations. I considered making a fantastic mobile, some unusual jewelry, Christmas ornaments, or a work of art. I began to imagine that my prolific crane folding would result in any number of new opportunities and that soon I could quit my job and become a master crane folder. When I had folded about seventy birds, I started to calculate how many cranes I could complete in an hour, how many hours I could devote per day, and how many days it would take to complete the folding of my one thousand cranes. But when I reached one hundred and fifty three cranes, my enthusiasm started to falter and I didn't fold another crane for a long time. I later realized that I had lost sight of the simple elegance of the task. Instead of staying present in the process and enjoying each and every crease and fold of paper, I had become obsessed with finishing what I had come to perceive as little more than a task. So, I stopped folding and thought about what I was really seeking from my crane folding.

My attempt to fold one thousand cranes helped me to discover the Zen qualities known as "mindfulness" and "no-mind." Mindfulness is being in the moment, focusing our attention in one place. Too often our attention is divided between different tasks: We open our mail while talking on the phone, we think about what we're going to make for dinner while driving home from work. Most of the time, we allow our attention to drift and wander where it will. Conscious attention comes from the intention to be present, and it requires that we constantly enforce our focus. When we do not disperse our

consciousness over varied terrain, but fully focus our attention on where we are or what we are doing, we feel more fully alive. In many traditions, the arts are used as paths to mindfulness, and can sometimes take us one step beyond mindfulness to the state of no-mind. No-mind is a quality of being in which we are so focused on what we are doing that we become one with the activity and disappear into it. No-mind is when we release our sense of self and merge with the creative potential of the universe.

Now, years later, I've started folding cranes again, but today I fold to find the spirit in the paper, and in myself. I am mindful of every mountain and valley fold, every pinch and pull of the paper. When each new crane is nearly complete, I gently blow into it, spread its wings, and watch it come to life with my breath. And, sometimes, I think I hear the rustling of folded paper hanging from trees and the whisper of prayers unfolding.

No
seed
ever
sees
the
flower.
—ZEN SAYING

In Shintoism, prayers are whispered into pieces of paper that are then tied to trees. Shintoists believe that every time the wind rustles the papers, the prayers are repeated.

Folding One Thousand Cranes

Lao Tzu, the Chinese philosopher and founder of Taoism, wrote in the *Tao-te Ching*: "A tower of nine stories begins with a heap of earth. The journey of a thousand miles starts from where one stands." But, one thousand is just a number. Feel free to fold any number of cranes or not to keep count at all. If you want to count, you might choose a number that has personal meaning to you. For example, you could fold forty cranes on your fortieth anniversary or thirteen cranes with your daughter on her thirteenth birthday.

Although the legend claims that if you fold one thousand origami cranes, your wish will come true, there are no rules when it comes to how we release our wishes and prayers to the universe. You can decide how many cranes you need to fold to honor your intention. However, whether you fold a few or one thousand cranes, try to remain mindful of the paper, the folding, and the cranes. The more attentive you are to the task at hand, the more receptive you will become to the sacred space that can be found in creativity.

Create Sacred Space

Find a place where you can work without distraction. Begin by centering yourself, lighting incense or a candle, or saying a prayer. If you are folding one thousand cranes with another person or a group, turn it into a communal meditation and make a collective wish.

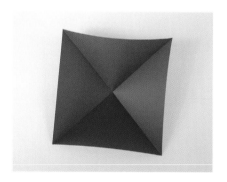

1. Fold a sheet of origami paper in half (color inside), corner to corner. Unfold and repeat with the opposite corners, to make an "x" pattern with "valley" folds.

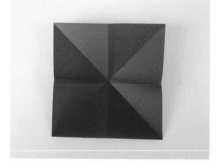

2. Turn the paper over and fold edge to edge with the color on the outside. Unfold and repeat with the opposite edges, to make a "+" pattern with "mountain" folds.

3. Refold the paper in half, with the color on the outside, along one of the mountain fold lines. Now hold the corners and start to bring together.

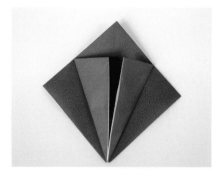

4. Complete the fold as shown above. You will have a form with four petal-like sides.

5. Collapse the folded paper.

6. Position the folded paper with the open end toward you. Now fold the outer edges of just the top flap toward the center crease so the top layer looks like a kite.

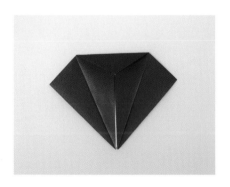

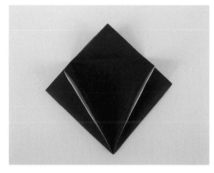

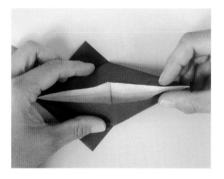

7. Fold down the top triangle of the kite shape.

8. Now unfold the three folds you made in Steps 6 and 7.

9. Turn the form sideways and lift up the top layer using the crease made in Step 6 as a hinge. Push on the "cheeks" of the form to flatten. Turn over and repeat.

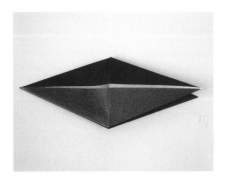

10. You should now have a long diamond shape on both sides. Carefully smooth your folds.

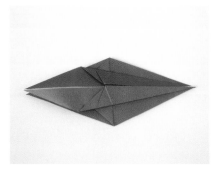

11. Orient the paper so that the split end with "legs" faces right. Now fold the outer edges of this end to meet the middle crease.

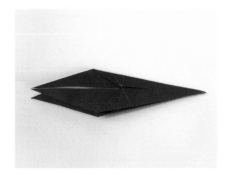

12. Turn over and repeat the Step 11 fold on this side so that the folded paper looks like a long, thin kite.

13. Position index fingers inside each leg and push the legs toward the center. Do this on both the front and the back of the folded form.

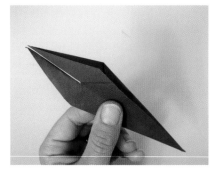

14. Now the form has short, separate "legs" at the top and a bottom that looks like a long triangle.

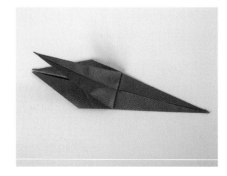

15. Lift up the top of the triangle layer along the existing crease.

16. Repeat on the other side. Now the form should look as shown.

17. Position your index fingers inside the folds as you did in Step 13, bringing the sides toward the front. Repeat on the other side.

18. Now you can see the tail and neck of the crane to come. Feel free to adjust the angle of the tail and neck to suit your taste.

19. To make the head, reverse fold as shown, tucking a little less than one inch of the neck into itself.

20. Open the wings and add a little curve to them if you wish.

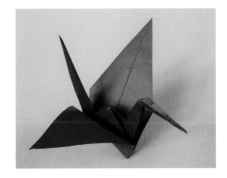

21. To inflate the crane, gently blow into the small hole on its underside while extending its wings. The crane is now complete.

INVITE THE SACRED TO PARTICIPATE
in your joy in little things, as well as in your
agony over the great ones. There are as many
miracles to be seen through a microscope as
through a telescope. Start with the little things
seen through the magnifying glass of wonder,
and just as a magnifying glass can focus the
sunlight into a burning beam that can set a leaf
aflame, so can your focused wonder set you
ablaze with insight.

—*Alice Howell*

Putting Our Hearts in Order
ZEN ROCK GARDENS

As I cleared the area I had designated for my Zen rock garden, I felt the endless potential of all the empty space. As Lao Tzu said, "We shape clay into a pot, but it is the emptiness inside that holds whatever we want." So it is with the Zen rock garden—we create it for the emptiness that it can hold. I had to sit with the vacant space for days before I could set the first stone into the earth. The emptiness taught me that there are endless possibilities in absence. It creates a clearing in which anything can take shape.

In the West, most of us do not picture the minimalist landscapes of Zen rock gardens when we hear the word "garden." Instead, we imagine lush and lively arrangements of plants and pathways designed to stimulate our senses. The Zen rock garden, in contrast, is created to soothe our spirits and calm our minds. This type of garden, known as *karesansui* in Japanese, is a flat space covered in a light-colored gravel that has been combed into patterns, such as concentric circles, waves, or parallel lines. The word, karesansui, is comprised of three Japanese root words, *kare:* "dry," *san:* "water," and *sui:* "mountain." Karesansui therefore describes a dry garden comprised of water and mountains, represented by gravel and stones.

In karesansui, rocks are set asymmetrically into the ground and surrounded by gravel. The rocks are typically dark shades, such as black and gray, so they stand out as a strong presence against the contrasting gravel. Plantings are minimal, limited to moss at the base of rocks and sometimes a

Only when
you have
no thing
in your mind
and no mind
in things
are you vacant
and spiritual,
empty
and marvelous.

—TE-SHAN/TOKUSAN

plant, shrub, or small tree positioned near a rock grouping. The feeling in a karesansui garden is one of emptiness. Space appears to reach out from the garden, infusing the surrounding world with a palpable stillness.

Karesansui has existed in Japan for centuries. Originally created primarily by Zen priests, karesansui uses rocks, gravel, and minimal plantings symbolically, to represent the teachings of Zen. It serves as a sanctuary for the mind as well as a work of spiritual art.

With its landscape of mountains and coastline, Japan has an abundance of rocky shores, cliffs, and river valleys covered with rocks and stones. The ancient Japanese believed that stones were the dwelling place of deities, called *kami*. The religion indigenous to Japan, called Shinto, involved the ceremonial worship of kami, the mysterious and sacred forces of nature that were believed to reside in stones, trees, springs, caves, mountains, cliffs, and other features of the landscape. Sacred sites were established by

creating enclosures around stones (and other elements of nature), and by spreading white gravel to consecrate the ground that surrounded them. These Shinto enclosures—considered a bridge between the sacred and the profane—served as early models for Japanese Zen gardens.

Zen practioners adapted the use of carefully positioned stones to express philosophical ideas. The arrangement of rocks became a highly developed art, as well as a spiritual exercise embodying the Japanese belief that stone arranging can "put the heart in order." Placed in a sea of gravel, a rock, or groupings of rocks, might represent a thought perfectly placed in the mind. The gravel in a Zen garden can represent the Buddhist concept of no-mind, which is a mind that can flow like the water evoked by the patterns raked into the gravel.

Eventually I did set my stones into the ground and then I surrounded them with gravel raked into patterns evocative of flowing water. But I

Karesansui—the Japanese word for dry landscape Zen gardens—is comprised of three root words, *kare*: "dry," *san*: "water," and *sui*: "mountain."

kept the garden simple and minimal, wanting to retain that open sense of expectancy I experienced when first contemplating the unadorned space. One of the principles of the Zen rock garden is to dispense with all superfluous elements, so that the garden invites us to empty ourselves of mental clutter. The garden is created to evoke a contemplative experience that can connect us with the living consciousness of creation. According to Zen practitioners, the original state of the human soul is one that allows us to experience the world spontaneously, in the moment, with a clear mind and an open heart. By emptying our minds, we can reconnect with that consciousness, recovering what feels absent, but is, in actuality, always present. Therefore, within the Zen tradition, we don't need to seek enlightenment because it already belongs to us. Perhaps in the empty space of a Zen garden we can put our hearts in order and rediscover what is already ours.

Nature can provide inspiration for stone setting.

Creating a Miniature Zen Rock Garden

We have created a scaled-down tabletop version of a Zen rock garden that will introduce you to the experience of karesansui.

What You Need

An unpainted shadow-box picture frame about 12 by 16 inches, with 2 inches or more in depth; a wooden board that fits inside the frame; wood glue; black paint; a paint brush; approximately 2 pounds of off-white craft sand (to use instead of gravel); stones of various shapes and sizes, appropriate to the scale of the garden; objects to use as rakes, such as combs, forks and other kitchen utensils, and branches.

Center

Before you begin, take a moment to sit quietly and empty your mind of distracting thoughts so that you can be fully engaged in the creation of the Zen garden.

Make the Tray

Place a generous line of glue around the inside of the frame and place the wooden board inside the frame. Put a weight on top of the board to keep it pressed against the frame while it dries. When dry, paint both the inside and outside of the tray with black paint. Let the paint dry for a day or two so the sand won't stick to it.

Once the tray has dried for a day or two you can begin to place the rocks.

A simple rake can be constructed with dowels and one-by-one pine.

Select and Arrange the Stones

Prior to adding the sand you need to select and "set," or arrange, the stones. For Zen gardeners, the shape of stones is important. Low, smooth stones can imbue a garden with repose and quiet an anxious mind, whereas standing and angular stones have a forceful energy that can awaken our spirits.

Arranging stones in groups takes just as much consideration as does the selection of individual stones. Stones are traditionally grouped together asymmetrically to suggest mountains, waterfalls, and islands. The numbers three, five, and seven are considered auspicious by Buddhists; therefore, many gardens have clusters of three, five, or seven rocks. The position of rocks can suggest pursuit or retreat, tension or serenity. Rocks—individually and in groupings—are sometimes used to represent cranes, tortoises, other animals, objects, and even Buddhas. The spaces in between and around rocks are as important as the positions of the rocks themselves. Remember, in a karesansui, the empty space has an energy all its own.

Add the Sand and Rake Patterns

Once the stones are in position, fill the tray with the sand so that you have a covering about an inch deep. From its use in Shinto shrines, white

Smaller stones can be placed on top of the sand to make island-like arrangements.

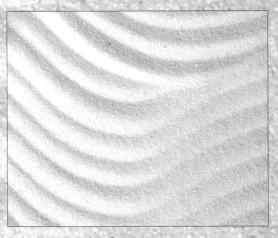

Raked sand evokes flowing water.

Zen Rock Gardens 117

gravel—represented by the white sand—indicates sacred ground, so it's used to consecrate the garden space.

You can make a simple rake with lumber scraps and wooden dowels or with branches found in nature. Or, you can use found objects.

Rake the sand into patterns, trying different types of rakes to see what kind of pattern most appeals to you. The raked sand adds texture as well as shadows—created by the grooves—to the garden. Gravel traditionally represents flowing water, so patterns are usually straight, wavy, or concentric. Grooves that are more widely spaced represent calmer water; more tightly spaced lines reflect the high energy of waves or tumbling water; and a combination of spacing might suggest a shifting tide or current. Unraked sand can evoke an open space or the sky.

Adding Other Elements

You can add other elements to the garden, but keep it simple. Remember, the Zen rock garden is based on the guiding principle that less is more. Other items to consider are very small beach stones or a tiny piece of driftwood.

Contemplating a Zen Rock Garden

Sit where you can comfortably contemplate the Zen garden—indoors or outdoors. You can set the garden outside on a sunny day as long as you bring it inside when you are finished with your contemplation. Allow the patterns of sand to slow down your entire being and let its emptiness still your mind. Breathe deeply and fully. Allow the rocks to speak to your soul and tell you their ancient secrets. Try to feel the kami, or spirits, that inhabit all things: the sand and stones, the sky and wind. Trust that your life, like the stones you have arranged, and the universe itself, is in perfect order.

Stories that Groups of Stones Can Tell

Rock groupings in a Zen garden sometimes represent fables. The groupings at the famous Zen garden at Ryoanji are believed to tell the tale of a tigress and her cubs. The tigress forced her seven cubs to swim across a river as a test of their courage. A Buddha who was watching became worried about the cubs' safety, so he dove into the water, sacrificing himself to save them. At another garden, the Temple of the Golden Pavilion at Rokuonji, the stone groupings tell the story of a carp that scaled a waterfall to become a dragon, who then flew to heaven.

The entire universe is concentrated in a garden.

—Sobin Yamada

JAPANESE GARDENS ASK THAT YOU GO

beyond the garden spiritually.

That you look at the garden not merely as an

object but also as a path into

the realms of the spirit.

—*Makoto Ooka*

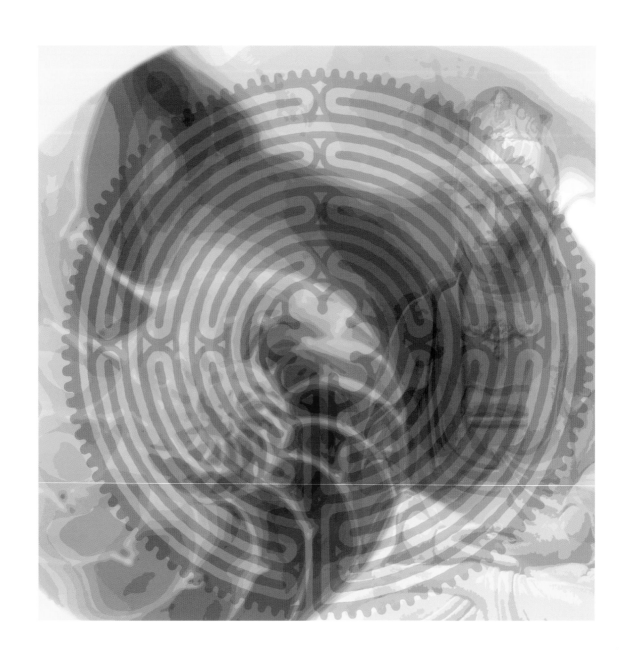

Coming Full Circle
WALKING A LABYRINTH

Most of us are familiar with the famous labyrinth from ancient Crete, the legendary lair of the Minotaur that Theseus slew with the help of Ariadne and her ball of thread. As the story is told, King Minos, ruler of Crete, angered the god Poseidon by not killing a bull intended for sacrifice. To punish Minos, Poseidon caused his wife, Queen Pasiphae, to be consumed with passion for the bull. From the union that ensued came the half-man, half-bull beast known as the Minotaur, which Minos kept confined in the center of a labyrinth. To keep the Minotaur fed, seven boys and seven girls from the other Greek states were sacrificed each year. One year, Theseus, son of the Athenian king Aegeus, volunteered to go to Crete, hoping to slay the beast and free his people from the annual sacrifice. When Theseus arrived in Crete, he won the love of Minos's daughter, Ariadne, who helped him navigate the labyrinth by giving him a ball of thread. Theseus tied one end of the thread to the entrance of the labyrinth and unraveled it as he made his way into the center. After slaying the Minotaur, he found his way out by following the thread.

The labyrinth I was about to enter, like the one in Crete, was unicursal, meaning it had only one path. Many people confuse the labyrinth and the maze, but a labyrinth is very different from a maze. A maze is multicursal—it's a walking puzzle that needs to be solved, with trick turns and dead ends, whereas a labyrinth is a single path that folds back on itself, continually changing direction until it reaches its center. Labyrinths do not have intersecting paths, therefore there are no choices to be made other than the choice to enter it. So, I made my choice and stepped inside.

One often sets an intention before walking a labyrinth, hoping the meditative exercise will stimulate insight and answers. My intention for walking the labyrinth was to gain clarity around some important decisions that I was facing. As I started walking, I tried to keep my heart open and mind empty, which isn't always easy. But, just as waves of thoughts would start to flood my consciousness and pull me away from the moment, I would approach a reverse turn that pulled me back to being present in the walk. It was as if the architecture of the labyrinth was trying to keep me focused. This is part of what the labyrinth is all about—it twists us back and forth until we've symbolically lost our way. Our temporary loss of orientation opens us to transformation, which is why so many cultures used the labyrinth in initiation rituals.

Since ancient times, the labyrinth has represented the meandering path of the soul through life, death, and rebirth. This symbolism may have originated in the labyrinth's similarity to the twisting paths that lead to and come from caves, which symbolize the womb. When Theseus walked the labyrinth, he was symbolically returning to the womb—the center of the labyrinth—where he discovered his true self by facing his demons, personified by the Minotaur. Theseus's walk through the labyrinth was a hero's journey, an initiatory test in which his old self died and a new self was born. Historically, the labyrinth so embodied this symbolism that it was widely depicted on tombs to represent the hope of rebirth after death.

For medieval Christians, walking the labyrinth was a ritual reminder that if they held onto their faith, they would not lose their way, but would be guided by God. Back in the late 1300s, the Anglo-Saxon word "clew" referred to a ball of thread. At that time, people used clews to thread their way out of garden labyrinths. The "threading" was a symbolic gesture that represented divine guidance. Eventually, the word "clew" evolved into "clue," and stood for something that guides us. But, in actuality, neither Theseus nor the medieval Christians needed Ariadne's ball of thread to keep from getting physically lost because it isn't possible to lose one's way in a labyrinth. There's only one way in and one way out, regardless of how many twists and turns occur along the path. Theseus may not have known that the invisible hand of destiny was guiding him, but he had the ball of thread—a visible clue—that gave him the confidence he needed to enter the labyrinth, slay the beast, and fulfill his destiny.

Theseus was lucky. The rest of us don't always have a clue. We usually walk life's labyrinths without a visible thread to guide us. Yet, that doesn't mean the thread isn't there—it is; it's just hard to see sometimes. When I was walking the labyrinth, I knew I would reach the center, but there were many times I felt more like the labyrinth was pulling me away from, rather than closer to, its center. The unexpected meandering away from the center reminds us of those times in life when our goals remain elusive despite our best efforts. Yet, it is in the moments of meandering that the labyrinth simultaneously symbolizes a temporary loss of hope as well as an invitation to have faith. Walking a labyrinth can help us accept where we are on our paths, especially during those times when we can't find our threads. The labyrinth reminds us that we are all exactly where we need to be at any given moment.

Sometimes I go about in pity for myself, and all the while a great wind is bearing me across the sky.
—Ojibwa Saying

Walking a Labyrinth

Three thousand years after Theseus unraveled Ariadne's thread, labyrinth-walking has become a popular spiritual practice, and more than five hundred labyrinths exist in North America alone. Because walking a labyrinth transcends religious traditions, one can find labyrinths at churches, schools, parks, hospitals, and community centers. The labyrinths are used as meditation tools that help us deepen our spirituality, access intuition and creativity, integrate the body and spirit, and identify obstacles that hold us back. Find a labyrinth in your area using the Website listed on page 134 or use the instructions starting on page 130 to make your own labyrinth from stones, bricks, or other path markers. You might also make a temporary labyrinth on the sand at the beach. If none of these options are available to you, use the tabletop labyrinth on page 133, adapting the suggestions that follow, as necessary.

Preparing to Walk a Labyrinth

Set your intention for the walk. You might want to meditate upon an aspect of your life, to receive guidance about a problem, or simply to open your heart and mind to inspiration. You might want to repeat a mantra during your walk. A mantra is a phrase, word, or sound that will help you focus your thoughts on your intention. Try not to have any expectations, so that you can remain open to whatever the experience offers. If others are walking the labyrinth at the same time you are, don't be distracted by their presence or pace, and remain respectful of theirs.

Beginning Your Walk

Silently stand at the entrance of the labyrinth and observe the path that opens before you. You might want to offer a prayer or blessing for the journey you are about to take. Then focus on your intention, and take your first step. If you have a mantra, silently repeat it as you take each step. Become aware of your feelings—emotional and physical—and allow them to guide your pace. You will be meandering back and forth, turning 180 degrees with each new circuit in the labyrinth's design. This changing of direction may disorient you slightly or cause your awareness to shift from the left brain to the right brain, possibly inducing a more receptive state of consciousness.

Continuing Your Walk

As you approach the center of the labyrinth, check in with yourself. How do you feel? Do you feel like slowing down to savor the last few steps or speeding up to get there sooner? If you are walking with others and need to wait to reach the center, be patient. You will arrive at the center when you are meant to. Once you arrive there, remain at the center for at least a few minutes, and even if you are walking with others, take some time to be still, and to empty your mind and receive whatever comes to you. When you are ready to begin the journey back out, you might want to offer a prayer of thanks and then refocus on your intention before you begin the return journey. If you are using a mantra, begin repeating it silently once again as you take the first step away from the center.

Coming Full Circle

As you walk along the path out of the labyrinth, remain focused on your intention. Since the entrance has now become the exit, let this be a reminder that all endings are beginnings and all beginnings are endings. As you conclude your walk, take another moment to be still and center yourself, offering a prayer or blessing just before you step out of the labyrinth.

Integrating Your Experience

After walking the labyrinth, you need to bring back any insights you may have gained during your walk to your normal state of awareness. Remember how you felt at different points along the path and relate those feelings to current situations in your life. Ask yourself how you can best integrate these discoveries into your everyday life.

*We shall not cease
from exploration
And the end of
all our exploring
Will be to arrive
where we started
And know the place
for the first time.*
—*T.S. Eliot*

Making a Labyrinth

If you can't find a labyrinth in your area or if you want regular access to one, it's easy to make a simple seven-circuit Cretan-style labyrinth. To determine the size requirements for a labyrinth, multiply the number of circuits (or paths) by the circuit width and then double that measurement (because the circuits repeat on both sides of the center). To this number add the width of path markers multiplied by the number of division lines.

For example, to make a seven-circuit labyrinth with a one-foot wide walking path with brick path markers:

7 circuits x 2 (to double) = 14 x 1 foot (width of walking path) = 14 feet

4 inches (width of brick path markers) x 15 (number of division lines)= 60 inches, or 5 feet

14 feet + 5 feet = 19 feet. So, you would need a circular space nineteen feet in diameter to make a seven-circuit labyrinth with one-foot wide paths marked by standard bricks.

What You Need
Measuring tape; stones, bricks, or other path markers.

1. Using path markers, make a 3' by 3' cross in the exact center of the labyrinth area. Now, add right-angle brackets between the arms of the cross, at least one foot away from the inside corners of the cross, to leave room for a walking path. From this point on, you will need to always leave a foot in between all division lines.

2. Now, place a path marker about one foot away from the inside of each bracket.

3. Use path markers to connect the vertical arm of the left bracket to the top of the central cross.

4. Connect the top left marker with the vertical arm of the top right bracket.

5. Connect the top right marker with the horizontal arm of the top left bracket.

6. Connect the left arm of the central cross to the horizontal arm of the top right bracket.

7. Connect the right arm of the central cross to the horizontal arm of the bottom left bracket.

8. Connect the bottom left marker to the horizontal arm of the bottom right bracket.

9. Connect the bottom right marker to the vertical arm of bottom left bracket.

10. Complete the labyrinth by connecting the bottom arm of the central cross to the vertical arm of the bottom right bracket.

Tabletop Labyrinth

Here is a labyrinth that you can follow with your finger. Enlarge the image on a photocopier. Follow the path with your finger just as you would if you were walking it, using the suggestions for the walking meditation.

Locate a Labyrinth in Your Area

At the Grace Cathedral Website, there is a link to the "Labyrinth Locator." Once there, simply enter your city and/or state to retrieve a list of labyrinths in your area. Many of the labyrinths listed are owned by churches or other non-profit organizations and getting permission to walk one is usually as simple as calling the phone number provided and asking when the labyrinth is open to the public.

http://www.gracecathedral.org/labyrinth/ locator/index.html

Where we had thought to travel outward, we will come to the center of our own existence. And where we had thought to be alone, we will be with all the world.

—Joseph Campbell

An aerial view of a labyrinth created by cutting prarie grasses. (The Prarie Labyrinth, Sibley, Missouri.)

I AM CIRCLING AND CIRCLING. . .

Am I a falcon,

a storm,

or a great song?

—*Rainer Maria Rilke*

PART THREE

The Path of
Prayer

Dispatching Prayers
THE ANDEAN *DESPACHO*

W e reached Chua Chua, a remote Q'ero village nearly 15,000 feet above sea level in the Peruvian Andes, hours before the pack horses carrying our warm clothes and gear arrived. Shivering, acutely aware of the altitude, and weary from sitting astride mountain ponies for the grueling seven-hour climb, we suddenly found ourselves feeling vulnerable in the harshness of this mountain climate. We were on our way to *Q'ollorit'i*, an annual sacred festival held at the base of the glacier at Apu Sinak'ara, a mountain located in southern Peru. Unlike the majority of the 70,000 pilgrims who travel to this festival via bus, car, or on foot, we were taking the high road, making the four-day trek through the isolated mountain passes on horseback, stopping at several Q'ero villages along the way.

The Q'ero are a Quechua-speaking indigenous people of south-central Peru. Due to the remoteness of their mountain villages, they have, until recently, had little contact with the Western world. This isolation has enabled them to preserve much of their ancient spiritual tradition and way of life. The Q'ero call themselves the "grandsons of Inkari"—the mythical first Inka—and are one of the few indigenous Andean groups who have retained the myths and knowledge of the Inca civilization. The Q'ero believe that everything in nature is animate and that we are in constant energetic interchange with the world of living energy. Embodied in this belief is the concept of *ayni*, or reciprocity. Ayni is similar to the familiar axiom, "Do unto others as you would have them do unto to you." Andeans practice this principle within their community, as well as in their interaction with the energies of

*As the crickets' soft
autumn hum is to us
so are we to the trees
as they are to the
rocks and the hills.*

— GARY SNYDER

Andean paqos preparing *despachos,* or, bundles of
ritually prepared offerings.

nature. The two major energies of the natural realm are the *Apus*, the spirits of the mountains, and the *Pachamama*, the spirit of the Earth. The Q'ero call upon the Apus for guidance and assistance, and rely upon the Pachamama for sustenance and livelihood. One of the ways the Q'ero reciprocate the generosity and guidance given them by a nature spirit is through the *despacho* ceremony, a perfect expression of ayni.

With the generous assistance of the villagers of Chua Chua, by way of a sack of warmed potatoes and a wind-tight shelter, we were able to find comfort until our gear arrived later that evening. A further demonstration of generosity

came when we were told that a despacho ceremony would be performed for us. The despacho is a ritually prepared bundle of natural and cultural objects of symbolic significance imbued with the maker's prayers. Literally translated, *despacho* means "dispatch," or a message of great importance sent with haste. Despachos can be made as offerings of thanksgiving or atonement, or as petitions for assistance or guidance. In our case, two Q'ero *paqos*—practitioners of the Andean spiritual arts—would prepare two despachos, one to the Apus and one to Pachamama, as prayers for our continued safe journey to Q'ollorit'i.

In the candlelit hut, the paqos opened the paper bundle containing the despacho items. Despacho bundles, or kits, contain all the ingredients one needs for creating this prayer offering, including a collection of between thirty and fifty *recados*—sacred items—wrapped in small pieces of paper. Recados include candy, cookies, seeds, stones, plant materials, llama fat, tiny squares of metallic paper, starfish arms, metal charms, and more. The kits are sold in the marketplace and are prepared for both general or specific purposes, such as attracting love or prosperity, or for healing.

The paqos began the ceremony by spreading a white piece of paper on the floor in front of them. On top of the paper they centered a scallop shell, in which they placed a small metal cross. They then sorted through a bag of coca leaves, collecting and arranging perfect leaves in sets of three, which are called *k'intus*. A k'intu was handed to each of us and we were told to blow our prayers into it and then chew the leaves.

The two paqos opened up the tiny paper packets containing the ritual items, peered at the contents, and conferred with each other. Sometimes they shook their heads and set the packet aside; other times they removed some of the contents and placed them carefully into the despacho. Once the paqos completed the first despacho to Pachamama, they began the second one, intended for the Apus. For this despacho,

A despacho comprised of k'intus surrounding a scallop shell

we handed the k'intus back to the paqos after we blew our prayers into them so that they could place them around the shell and cross. Then they began adding the recados to the despacho. Three hours later, when they were satisfied with the despachos, the paqos folded the papers around their contents and secured each bundle with string. They then wrapped the despachos together in a woven cloth and sprinkled the bundle with an offering of the strong Andean alcohol called *pisco*. They breathed their blessings into the bundle and passed it to each of us to do the same. The two paqos later released the despachos by burning the bundles in the cooking fire. Apparently their, and our, prayers were heard, for we arrived safely at Q'ollorit'i several days later.

A paqo making two despachos

Making an Andean Despacho

*More things are
wrought by prayer
than this world
dreams of.*

—Alfred Lord
Tennyson

An Andean paqo spends years training in the preparation of despachos, learning about the symbolism of the despacho contents. In the Andes, you can purchase a despacho kit and a pouch of coca leaves at the market. However, in most countries possession of coca leaves, a plant sacred to the Andean people, is illegal, and the contents of the despacho kit would not likely pass the agricultural restrictions of Customs. But since these items are symbolic, we can make our own despachos, or prayer packets, by substituting similar items from our own culture. Therefore, when making your despacho, simply choose items that hold special significance for you. Like the Q'ero, you can perform this ceremony alone or with a group, and your intention for the despacho can be individual or collective. Here are some suggestions for preparing your own despacho.

What You Need

Select items that represent your intention for the despacho. For example, include photographs or representations of people you may be praying for, a bit of soil from a place that is special to you, or a sprig of rosemary because it holds personal symbolic meaning. Include herbs, flowers, and other items related to the purpose of your despacho. If you are going to use k'intus, bay leaves are good substitutes for coca leaves.

Select a piece of paper sized to accommodate your despacho and remember that it will need to be large enough to wrap around the contents. You can also make a tiny despacho that can be carried in your pocket, enclosed in a card to a friend, or released to the wind on a mountaintop. Simply adjust the size of the despacho materials to make a smaller packet.

Create Sacred Space

Light a candle, smudge the area, or say a prayer. Prepare yourself mentally to be completely present and intent on what you are doing and why.

Despacho materials

Assemble the Despacho

Place a sheet of paper in the center of your work area. If you are going to use k'intus, make them by placing three bay leaves together, one on top of another. Choose leaves that are as perfect as possible. Holding the k'intu in both hands, blow your prayers into it and then place it in the center of the paper. If you are performing this ceremony with a group, each participant can work with a k'intu. Generally, twelve k'intus are used in a despacho to the Apus (because there are twelve major Apus surrounding the Sacred Valley of Peru), but feel free to adapt the number to something meaningful to your purpose. K'intus can be placed in a circle around the center of the paper. Once all the k'intus have been placed, you can begin adding other items to the despacho.

You may want to write your wishes or prayers on a piece of paper that you will place in the despacho. You may also want to use images that embody the intent of your despacho. For example, if you are hoping to travel to Spain, you might want to include a small map of the country in your despacho.

Make it beautiful—Andean despachos are natural works of art. Allow yourself to be creative. Use handmade or printed papers, powdered

A despacho before wrapping

A completed despacho, sealed with wax

The Andean Despacho 143

incense, or flower petals. During your assembly of the despacho, arrange the items in an aesthetically pleasing pattern, such as a mandala.

You can also lightly sprinkle the despacho with wine, perfume, or another liquid that is meaningful to you throughout the creation of the despacho.

Completing the Despacho

When you are finished, wrap the paper around the contents, and then tie the package with string or yarn. For smaller versions, use colorful thread or a band made from a thin strip of paper. Add a sprig of sage, feather, or other item to the outside of the despacho. You might want to seal the despacho with sealing wax and a seal related to your intention.

Releasing the Despacho

Once you have completed your despacho, decide how you want to "release" it. Does it feel right to burn it, bury it, let the wind carry it (if it is very small), or the water take it? Choose what feels right for the intent of your despacho. Placing it in the earth can represent gestation, releasing it to the water can be purifying, and burning it can be transforming. Whatever method you choose, always be conscious of the environment and safety.

Finally, try to release your expectations about how your prayer might be answered. The universe works in mysterious ways and rarely do things happen in the exact way that we envision. As Buddha said: "Faith is the beginning of all good things."

SYMBOLISM OF ANDEAN DESPACHO CONTENTS

Shell for feminine Energy
Cross for masculine Energy
Red flowers for the Pachamama (earth)
White flowers for the Apus (mountains)
Sweets for the earth spirits

Nuts & Grains for mountain spirits
Seeds for germination, growth, and potential
Color silver for feminine energy
Color gold for masculine energy

In the Andes, you can purchase a despacho kit containing traditional materials. But since these items are symbolic, you can make your own despachos by substituting items that hold special significance for you.

ASK, AND IT WILL BE GIVEN YOU;

search, and you will find;

knock, and the door

will be opened for you.

Matthew 7:7

Prayer in Motion
PRAYER FLAGS

Mysterious, invisible, and boundless, wind travels everywhere, slowed by topographic features, changed by fluctuating temperatures and latitudinal variations, but essentially unstoppable. Every day, somewhere on Earth, countless members of the plant kingdom send their seeds off on the wind to settle elsewhere and perpetuate their species. One great flurry of wind carries a cloud of milkweed seeds far from home; a burst of spring breeze propels thousands of helicoptering maple seeds to new terrain; and an early summer gust through a pine forest sends off trillions of specks of pollen to fertilize a new generation of trees.

Just as plants rely on the wind to scatter their seeds, Tibetans employ the wind to disperse their prayers. Prayer flags are flown all over the Tibetan world—on mountains and roof-tops, at monasteries, from bridges—almost anywhere the wind is likely to catch them. When wind blows through the flags, the prayers inscribed on them are carried as blessings to all beings. Tibetans aspire to spread goodwill and harmony to all, so what better mode of transportation than the unstoppable wind?

The Tibetan word for prayer flag is *Lung ta*, meaning "wind horse." Wind horse is a symbol of strength and freedom from fear that represents a transformative state of mind with the power to turn obstacles into advantages. Tibetans believe that people with strong wind horse have good fortune, and all things in their lives go well, whereas those with low wind horse tend to have more troubles in their lives. If a Tibetan is experiencing low wind horse, a *lama*, or priest, may suggest that he or she hang prayer flags.

149

Prayer flags are generally printed from wood block designs on colorful pieces of cotton, which are then cut into banners and strung together. Traditionally, flags are made in five colors, each representing one of the five elements—blue signifies space; white signifies water; red signifies fire; green signifies air and wind; and yellow signifies earth. In the corners of most flags, the names of four powerful animals are written—the garuda, a magical, mythical bird representing wisdom; the dragon, representing gentle power; the snow lion, representing fearless joy; and the tiger, representing confidence. However, on most flags the central image is a horse—the wind horse—who bears three flaming jewels on its back. The three jewels symbolize the Buddha; the dharma, or Buddhist teachings; and the sangha, or Buddhist community. Surrounding the wind horse are auspicious symbols, invocations, prayers, and mantras. These powerful symbols and inscriptions are dedicated to a particular deity or are more general prayers for long life and good fortune. An example of a prayer that might be found on a prayer flag is "May all live an authentic presence, in dignity, in happy circumstances and thus live a life of harmony fulfilling all wishes."

Tibetan Buddhists believe that the wind passes over the surface of the flag, consecrating and harmonizing the air with the writings and symbols that are inscribed on it. The prayers, like seeds, are then carried by the wind to infinite destinations, blessing everything they touch. The dissemination of prayer and good wishes grows exponentially because all those who come into contact with the prayer-imbued wind then spread the blessings to all who they contact, and so on.

Prayer flags hanging from Swayambunath Temple, Katmandu, Nepal

Through their acts of compassion and peace, Tibetan Buddhists hope to help others move forward on a path to enlightenment. Because the flags send prayers all over the Earth, by virtue of the pervasive wind, hanging flags is one way that a Buddhist can help many people at one time.

Of course, ultimately the flags deteriorate in the elements. However, even the fading of the images on the prayer flags is seen as evidence that the blessings are being carried by the wind and released into the world.

For the past week, the autumnal wind has been gusty and strong, and the leaves are falling from the trees in great bursts of orange and yellow. I had hung prayer flags on my porch about a month ago, and I have been watching them flutter in the unrelenting wind ever since. Each time I look at them, I am reminded that my prayers are gliding with the air currents in shimmering streams. Like the seeds that are carried away to a million places, promising new generations of plant life, these prayers are drifting all over the world, casting their blessings as far as the wind can travel.

May we all achieve the glory of virtue which will be just as white as a lilylike moon.

—Traditional Prayer Flag Blessing

Prayer flags at Bodnath, Nepal

Another Way to Use Motion to Pray: Prayer Wheels

The Tibetan Prayer Wheel, or *mani* wheel, is another way in which Tibetans use motion to release prayer. Prayer wheels can be small enough to hold in your hand or so large that they are installed in monasteries, temples, and other locations. The hand-held prayer wheel is constructed of a cylinder made of metal or leather mounted on a handle. At the base of the cylinder is the design of a lotus, and on the top part of the cylinder is an eight-spoked wheel signifying the dharma, the teachings of Buddha. Within the cylinder, the mantra, or chant, *Om Mani Padme Hum*, is printed on paper or cloth numerous times and wound around a spindle.

This mantra literally means the "Om, the Jewel in the Lotus, Hum!" and symbolizes the union of method and wisdom in attaining enlightenment. Each time the wheel is turned clockwise, prayers are released. The person turning the wheel also chants the prayers, which increases their release. Larger prayer wheels are sometimes placed in streams, in high places, or near a source of heat, so their prayers are released through the power of the water, wind, or fire. Tibetan Buddhists believe that by using a prayer wheel you can purify negative karma and travel farther down the path toward enlightenment.

Prayer wheels and pilgrims, Sakya Monastery, Bhutan

Making and Hanging Prayer Flags

Hanging prayer flags is a collaboration with nature: The ritual relies on the wind—a symbol of spiritual power from the heavens—to carry prayers and blessings all over the world. Expand the collaboration by making and hanging prayer flags with others. As prayer flags are usually hung in multiple numbers, each participant can create one or more flags and then the flags can be strung together and hung.

What You Need

Cotton cloth cut into approximately 8 by 10 inch rectangles; cord; fabric markers, fabric paint, or textile ink (which can be applied with brushes); sewing needle; thread; paper; masking tape; iron; old cutting board; pushpins.

Set Your Intention

Before you begin, sit quietly for a few minutes and think about your intention for the flags. Close your eyes and allow images that represent your intention to come to mind. Open your eyes, and if you would find it helpful, sketch the images you visualized on a sheet of paper.

Sewing the Flags

Fold over one inch of fabric at one of the short ends of the flags, iron the fold, and sew a hem, leaving enough room for threading the cord (Figure 1). Do this for each flag.

Designing the Flags

Draw the symbols, statements, and/or designs that reflect your intention with a pencil. You can use the wind horse template on page 159 if you would like to manifest strength, freedom from fear, and good fortune. Either copy it freehand or photocopy the template. If you want to trace either the wind horse and/or the images that you sketched after your visualization, you can use a lightbox, or you can tape the template (or sketch) onto a sunny window using masking tape. Then tape the fabric on top of the image. The sunlight should allow you to see the image through the fabric.

After you have traced or drawn your design in pencil, it's time to make it permanent with

Figure 1: The hemmed flag

fabric paint or markers. Or, alternatively, you can work without a sketch and add color to the flags freehand. First, however, you need to tack the flag onto a scrap of wood or old cutting board to keep it taut while drawing or painting. You may want to put paper towels in between the board and the flag to absorb excess paint or ink. When you are finished drawing or painting on your flags, hang them until they are completely dry, following the specific instructions of the paint or marker manufacturer.

Stringing the Flags

Once the flags are dry, you need to string them together. Cut a length of cord or rope based upon how many flags you are going to string together. Include a little space between each flag

and about three feet on each end to allow you to tie the ends to supports, such as porch posts or two trees. Thread the cord through the hem of the flags (Figure 2) and then tack the flags into position with a few stitches so they stay in place on the cord (Figure 3).

Hanging the Flags

When hanging your prayer flags, begin by creating a sacred atmosphere. Tibetans usually burn incense while hanging their flags. Choose a hanging location that is out in the open, where the wind moves freely, such as high on a hill, between trees, or on a deck, porch, or fire escape. Securely tie the string of flags over a distance so it creates a span, as you will want the wind to blow over all the flags.

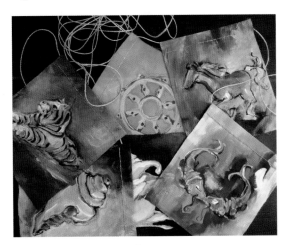

Figure 2: Threading the flags

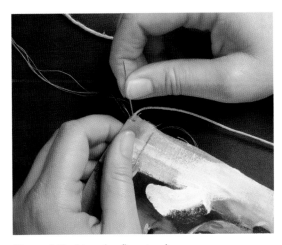

Figure 3: Tacking the flags in place

Awaken and listen,
you solitary ones!
Winds are coming
from the future
with mysteriously
beating wings,
and good news
is reaching
sensitive ears.

—FRIEDRICH
NIETZSCHE

A string of flags

When the Flags Fade

After a period of time, the flags will become faded and tattered. You can leave them in place until they are completely deteriorated or you can burn them ceremonially to complete the release of your prayers.

Inauspicious Days

According to Tibetan astrology there are two days of each Tibetan month when hanging prayer flags should be avoided; these are considered inauspicious days, bringing obstacles instead of success. The Tibetan calendar identifies inauspicious days as follows:

- The 10th and 22nd of the first, fifth, and ninth months
- The 7th and 19th of the second, sixth, and tenth months
- The 4th and 16th of the third, seventh, and eleventh months
- The 1st and 13th of the fourth, eighth, and twelfth months

These dates are based upon the Tibetan New Year, which is not a fixed holiday, so you need to count the months based on when it falls each year. You can find this information in a library or on the Internet.

Wind Horse Prayer Flag Template

MAY ALL BEINGS EVERYWHERE
with whom we are inseparably interconnected,
be fulfilled, awakened, liberated, and free.
May there be peace in this world
and throughout the entire universe,
and may we all together
complete the spiritual journey.

—*Mahayana Buddhist Prayer*

The Art of Impermanence
PAINTING WITH SAND

Even before we began the sand painting, we were already thinking about how difficult it would be to let it go when it was completed. We wondered how we would feel when it was time to take the brush and sweep the sacred work of art into a pile of sand. Before we could fully commit to creating the sand painting, we had to release these thoughts—and with some effort we succeeded. We respected that the essence of impermanence—one of the Three Marks of Existence in Buddhism—is the way of the Tibetan sand-painting ritual.

Dul-tson-kyil-khor, which means "mandala of colored powders," is the Tibetan word for the Tantric Buddhist ritual of sand painting. In this ceremony, Tibetan monks painstakingly create an intricate mandala—a sacred, geometric form of art—entirely with colored sand. The ritual begins long before the first grains of sand are patiently applied. Performed as an act of healing for an individual, the environment, a community, or the world—and undertaken in public or private—the monks begin the ritual with a blessing, invoking the power of goodness through music or by chanting mantras. Only following this consecration of the space do the monks actually begin creating the sand painting.

The monks first draw the mandala design on a wooden platform. Mandalas traditionally include intricate and often symmetrical designs of geometric shapes, the figures of deities, and depictions of sacred or spiritual icons. When the design is complete, the monks begin the sand painting itself, using a metal funnel called a *chak-pur* to direct thin streams of colored sand. The sand painting slowly

To see a world
in a grain of sand
And a heaven
in a wild flower,
Hold infinity
in the palm
of your hand
And eternity
in an hour.

—WILLIAM BLAKE

takes shape as they delicately tap the chak-pur to place the sand with amazing accuracy and infinite patience. The monks begin at the center of the mandala and work outward, symbolizing through their progress the ever-growing and ever-changing nature of the cosmos, from the smallest atom to the entire universe. They work in a state of silent meditation, and the painting can take days, or even weeks, to complete. This sacred painting is not only rich in spiritual meaning, it also can help heal those for whom it is created.

But a sand painting, no matter how long it takes to make, is short-lived, for it is created to be destroyed. As patiently as they created it, the monks now sweep the painting inward from the edge of the mandala toward its center. This destruction symbolizes the return of

Monks drawing a sand mandala

all things to their source, mirroring the impermanence of existence. Once the mandala is nothing more than a phantom image in the mind's eye, the pile of swirled sand is collected in an urn. Small portions of the sand may be given to guests for healing purposes, but most

of it is taken to the ocean or a river and released into the water—where the current will carry away the monks' prayers along with the grains of sand, dispersing them throughout the world.

As we began this ritual ourselves, we understood, intellectually, the concept of impermanence—that change is the only constant. In practice, however, we, like many others, struggle in the most personal of ways when confronted with change. We become attached to circumstances, relationships, ideas, and beliefs because they give us comfort and allay our fears. We wrestle profoundly and painfully to hold on to things, people, and ideas because we perceive them to be immutable. But deep inside we recognize the illusion, and must admit that everything—including our own physical existence—is transitory and mutable. According to certain schools of Buddhism, suffering arises when we resist the law of change. Instead, it is through acceptance of impermanence that we find the still center from which we can fully value each moment of

Tibetan sand mandalas traditionally include intricate and often symmetrical designs of geometric shapes, the figures of deities, and depictions of sacred or spiritual icons.

*Everything
changes,
nothing
remains
without
change.*

—BUDDHA

our lives. It is an enlightened mind that remembers that every change and loss gives birth to gifts as yet unimagined.

And so we began the ritual. First, we burned a little incense and took a moment to center, then we stated our intention for the sand painting, which was a prayer for world peace. Fully settled into the sacred space we had created, we began applying the sand. We found the process of painting with sand immensely satisfying. From the way the sand flowed out of our homemade chak-purs, making a sound like very light, dry snow falling on frozen ground, to the colorful pattern of the expanding mandala against the black background, the creation appealed thoroughly to our senses. We discovered that tapping the hand that held the chak-pur in the rhythmic beat of galloping horses created the perfect vibration for getting the sand to flow. As we completed each concentric shape, we admired the evolving form of the painting. It really didn't look like sand at all, but more like a beautifully quilted fabric.

When our painting was complete, we contemplated it while sipping cups of tea. We considered keeping it intact for a few days so we could continue to admire it, but we ultimately decided that doing so would defeat the purpose of releasing our prayer, and that we would be succumbing to attachment. Sweeping it up was initially difficult: Neither of us wanted to be the first to destroy it. But once we had brushed the first corner in, the painting began to metamorphose into a new form of beauty. The more we swept it inward, the more it changed into new colors and patterns. When the painting had been completely deconstructed and relinquished to a vase, we realized that it was somehow still whole within the container, just in another form.

A few weeks later, we took the vase of sand to the ocean and cast the mandala into the outgoing tide. As the swirls of colored sand floated on the water, our painting took on yet another form. But it lingered only briefly in the moving water before the surf dispersed it throughout the sea—a final metaphor of impermanence. With our prayer for peace released to the sea, we detached from the outcome, trusting that it would manifest in whatever form it needed to. The lessons of our sand painting were well taught: Do not resist the flow of change, welcome the unfolding of what is born in every new moment, and always engage in the relentless, but freeing practice of letting go.

Your work is to discover your work and then with all your heart to give yourself to it.
— BUDDHA

Monks make a sand painting by releasing just a few grains of sand at a time.

Where the Gods Come and Go

Tibetan Buddhism isn't the only tradition that practices the ritual of sand painting. Diné (or Navajo) sand painting, or *iikaah*, which means "place where the gods come and go," is a similar sacred art. It is used in healing ceremonies to restore balance, or *hozho*. The Diné believe that misfortune, accidents, bad luck, and illness are caused when an individual is out of balance. The Diné practice more than fifty different types of healing rituals and chants. These healing rituals can last anywhere from one to nine days.

During a Diné healing ceremony, the chanter, or medicine person, creates a sand painting on the floor of the ceremonial space. The images depicted include *Yei*—creation beings—healing plants, and natural phenomena such as rainbows, the sun, or stars. The designs are specifically chosen according to the particular ceremony being conducted. Once the sand painting is complete, the patient lies upon the painting and the restoration of harmony begins. The healer may take sand from various parts of the painting and rub it on the patient's body to absorb the energy of the imbalance. At the end of each day, when the ceremony is complete, the sand painting is destroyed.

A design depicting a Yei, or Diné creation being

Painting With Sand

The ritual of sand painting can be practiced alone or with others. Generally, unless the sand painting is going to be very large, a group shouldn't exceed four people. If you are interested in practicing the ritual with a larger group, divide yourselves into pairs or small groups of three or four people.

When drawing the pattern for your sand painting, try to use symbols that hold meaning for you. You might want to look at the Mandala Symbolism Chart on page 85 for some ideas on using color, number, and shape symbolism in your design.

Keep in mind that the intricately beautiful sand paintings created by Tibetan monks are the result of many years of training and practice. As you set out to create your first sand painting, keep your design simple. Finally, remember that the intention of your sand painting is more important than how perfectly it turns out. After all, it's not meant to be a lasting piece of art, but only an impermanent representation of your prayer.

What You Need
Black foam board or other rigid black board; white pencil; straight edge; compass; protractor; plastic straws (you will need half a straw to use as a chak-pur for each color of sand); eye droppers (you will need one for each chak-pur); plastic cups or other containers; colored sand; paper plates.

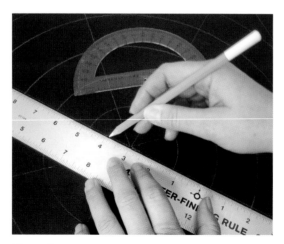

Figure 1

Figure 2

Center and Create Sacred Space

Take a moment to center yourself. You might want to light a candle or burn incense. State your prayer or intention for the sand painting, and try to be mindful of your intention throughout the ritual.

Draw the Guidelines

Cut the board into a square that measures 20 by 20 inches for a painting surface. Find the center of the square by drawing diagonal lines from corner to corner. After you've found the center—where the diagonal lines intersect—use a white pencil and compass to draw as many circles as you want. To section the circles, divide 360 by the desired number of sections to determine the degree measurement of each section.

For example, for a circle with 16 sections, divide 360 by 16 to arrive at 22.5 degrees. Then, use a protractor to measure and mark intervals of 22.5 degrees. Now, draw lines that intersect the degree marks (Figure 1). After sectioning the circles, you can add figures or other geometric shapes and designs. Alternately, you can simply draw a square or circle and apply the sand spontaneously, designing as you go.

Make the Chak-purs

Cut the straws in half and then cut one end of each half at a diagonal. The diagonally cut end will be the scoop. Remove the rubber bulbs from the eyedroppers (and discard the bulbs). Insert the straight-cut end of each straw into an eyedropper so that it fits snugly (Figure 2). Each

Hands
to
work,
hearts
to
God.
—SHAKER SAYING

Figure 3

Figure 4

It is not what we do,
it is how much love
we put out
in the doing.

—MOTHER TERESA

person who will be working on the sand painting will need one homemade chak-pur for each color of sand. Fill plastic cups or other containers with the sand so that you can easily scoop sand with the straw end of the chak-pur. You might want to place the cups of sand on paper plates to catch sand that is spilled as you work.

Painting with Sand

Select the color you will use first and fill your chak-pur with the sand by using the scoop end (Figure 3). Hold the chak-pur in your dominant hand as you would a pen or pencil. Now, tap the hand holding the chak-pur, or the chak-pur itself, with your other hand (Figure 4). This vibration will get the sand flowing. You should practice using the chak-pur so you can get a feel for how it works. For example, practice to gauge how fast the sand comes out when holding the chak-pur at different angles or how hard you need to tap to get the sand flowing. Begin your sand painting in the center and work outward. Not only is this the traditional way of working, but it will also minimize the risk that you'll disturb portions of your painting that have already been completed. Applying the sand could take a few hours to a few days depending upon the intricacy of your design. If a group is creating the sand painting, each person may need to work individually or a few at a time.

As the sand painting takes shape, enjoy its constantly changing beauty.

Sweeping Up and Letting Go

As hard as it is to imagine, once the sand painting is finished, you will need to destroy it. Sit with the finished painting or meditate upon it, allowing its beauty to resonate through you. When you are ready, use a soft brush to "unmake" it, beginning at the outside edges and sweeping the sand in toward the center until you have a tiny mountain of colored sand. Then mindfully scoop the sand into a container. If you want to, you can save a little of the sand as a symbol of the prayer or intention you held during the sand painting's creation. Then take the sand to a river or the ocean, cast it into the water, and watch as your prayers are carried out into the world.

When creating your sand painting, use symbols and shapes that hold personal meaning for you or that relate to the intention, or prayer, behind the sand painting.

LET GO OF THE PAST,

let go of the future,

and let go

what is in between,

transcending the things of time.

—*The Dhammapada*

Seeking What the Heart Holds Sacred
PILGRIMAGE

A s an inveterate seeker, I have been on pilgrimage for most of my adult life. I have been called to search for the things that matter to me in the eternal return of the ocean's surf, the thin air above timberline, the quiet, hidden life of deserts, and the mystery of time in history's vine-covered ruins. Sometimes the call to the road is gently persuasive; other times it is insistent. However it comes, the call is answered only by leaving my ordinary life and traveling to the destination that has summoned me. When I embark upon these journeys, I cross the threshold into sacred space and time, where my experiences range from awe-inspiring to deeply conflicting. And always, when I complete the circle by returning home with the experiences of the road in hand, I discover that my life has been somehow changed.

Whenever I think about what it means to go on a pilgrimage, I recall the eighth-century parable about a poverty-stricken rabbi from Cracow who had a recurring dream about a treasure buried near a bridge in Prague. Because his dream was persistent, he was compelled to travel in search of the treasure. When he arrived at the bridge, he discovered that it was heavily guarded, but having traveled so far, the rabbi lingered in the area waiting for his chance to search for the treasure. After several days, a guard approached him and demanded to know the nature of his business. Discouraged, the rabbi reluctantly revealed his dream and that he was there to search for the treasure. The guard admonished him, but then told him that he, too, had a recurring dream of a treasure, only in his dream, the treasure was buried under the hearth at the house of a poor rabbi in Cracow. The guard assured the rabbi,

For where your treasure is, there will your heart be also.

—Matthew 6:21

however, that he wasn't foolish enough to go hunting for a treasure just because it appeared in a dream. Upon hearing the guard's tale, the rabbi became exuberant, hurried home, and, sure enough, under his hearth, he discovered an immense treasure. The message of this parable reminds us that the sacred we seek is already within our hearts, but sometimes, in order to recognize it, we need to travel away from the familiar. This is the essence of pilgrimage—an inner restlessness that calls us away from home, to search for what the heart holds sacred.

Historically, a pilgrimage was a meditative journey, usually undertaken with austerity, to a sacred place. For some, a pilgrimage was an act of discipline or prayer, a way to acquire merit before God or to fulfill a vow. Sometimes, the journeys were obligatory, imposed upon the faithful by belief, as with the Muslim *hajj* to Mecca. For others, like those

who undertook the arduous journey to Santiago de Compostela, in Spain, pilgrimage was a matter of doing penance for crimes or sins committed. Medieval pilgrims who journeyed to Canterbury embarked upon the pilgrimage to touch relics and holy places, for communion with the divine, or for healing. Hindu mystics and Sufis believe that the journey to the sacred can be one that takes the pilgrim inward; therefore, they didn't always travel to distant lands, but sometimes journeyed metaphorically through meditation and prayer. Similarly, early Christians walked cathedral labyrinths, which were symbolic journeys to the sacred. Regardless of the traditions and destinations, all pilgrimages were undertaken to bring the pilgrim closer to a state of grace. Real or metaphoric, a pilgrimage had, and still has, the purpose of finding something that holds profound significance to the traveler, culminating in a deepened

The Borobudur shrine is an initiatory Buddhist edifice, to be ascended level by level by those seeking enlightenment. The lower levels, comprised of pagodas, *stupas*, and niches, lead to a single stupa at the top, symbolizing a path from multiplicity to oneness. Buddhist pilgrims circumambulate their way to the highest level in a clockwise direction so they can keep their right hands in contact with the shrine.

spiritual state or personal transformation.

Today, the reasons for taking a pilgrimage are not so different. We still seek those places that speak to our hearts, but these are not always the tombs of saints or the sites of miracles. These days, we often seek the sacred in places of profound natural beauty, cultural diversity, or historical significance. Sometimes, we know exactly what we're looking for; other times we have a longing we can't explain until it's fulfilled. Recently, while hiking in a canyon in the Southwest, I found myself enveloped in a silence so profound I could almost hear my cells dividing. I never experience that kind of quiet where I live, and I felt as if I could have stayed there forever, submerged in the silence as I gathered stones from a dry river bed. I hadn't realized how much my soul had longed for silence until I discovered it on that pilgrimage.

Sometimes, we set out on a pilgrimage with a very specific goal in mind only to discover that what we need isn't exactly where—or what—we thought it was. For example, years ago, I

undertook a journey with the intention of exploring the spiritual traditions of the Q'ero people of Peru. At first I found myself disappointed at the depth of cultural assimilation that had occurred in such a remote location. After all, there I was in the Q'ero villages, high in the Andes, yet I repeatedly encountered aspects of Christianity— a faith I associated more with my own culture than that of the Q'ero people. But later, at the festival of *Q'ollurit'i*, 16,000-feet-high in the mountains, I had an epiphany. I was watching a group of dancers perform before a *huaca*, or sacred shrine—in this case an enormous stone cross. When the fervor of the music stopped, everyone fell to their knees in an expression of devotion so powerful that I was moved to tears. In that moment, I finally understood that spirit can wear many guises, and how it manifests is not nearly as important as that it does manifest.

As the saying goes, it's not the destination, but the journey that matters most. One of the pleasures of a pilgrimage can be the fellow pilgrims we meet along the way. Chance encounters between kindred spirits can sometimes provide the answers we seek. Just as in ordinary life, on a pilgrimage we often find what we most need for ourselves by sharing with others. While staying at a small inn near Santa Fe, I lingered over coffee one morning with other guests and the innkeepers. It wasn't long before we spontaneously started sharing personal stories. We learned about one another's leaps of faith, times of doubt, triumphs, and losses. There, in the desert, a group of total strangers bonded and helped one another discover what they were looking for.

At the end of every pilgrimage there is always the challenge of returning home and integrating the extraordinary into the ordinary. If, in the chaos of daily life, I can hold onto the silence I found hidden in the canyon; if, in the middle of a traffic jam, I can feel the rapture I experienced high in the Andes; and if, on a crowded train on which no one meets my eyes, I can recall the intimate conver-

sations I've shared with strangers, then I know that my journeys have served me well. And, like the rabbi from Cracow, I realize that the sacred I sought was in my heart all along, and I just needed the ritual of the road to discover the treasures within.

Even in ancient times, people wrote guides for pilgrims, instructing the traveler where to go, how to behave, and what to avoid. These were the precursors to today's travel guides, which provide us with hotel and restaurant ratings, museum hours, parking fees, and the like. Although these guides can provide practical information, they don't tell us how to travel with an open heart and how to find the sacred in our journeys. You will need to do this for yourself. So, in all your travels, heed your callings, commit to your journey, and discover what is sacred to you. Celebrate the wonder you hold in your heart as you quest. Make your encounters vibrant with meaning and invest your experience with your heart and soul.

It is good to have an end to journey towards; but it is the journey that matters in the end.
—Ursula K. LeGuin

All the answers are within us, but such is our tendency toward forgetting that we sometimes need to venture to a faraway land to tap our own memory.

—HEINRICH ZIMMER

Reclining Buddha, Northern Thailand

Famous Sacred Pilgrimages

SANTIAGO DE COMPOSTELA, SPAIN

The Camino de Santiago is a thousand-year-old, five-hundred-mile-long pilgrim road across northern Spain. The journey culminates at the church of Santiago de Compostela (Saint James of the Star Field), where the relics of the apostle St. James are said to lie. Medieval pilgrims carrying scallop shells to identify themselves usually made this journey to redeem themselves before God.

MECCA, SAUDI ARABIA

The Koran instructs all Muslims to make the pilgrimage, or hajj, to Mecca, the spiritual center of Islam, at least once in their lives provided they can afford it. Here, the sacred actions of the prophet Mohammed are repeated. About three million pilgrims travel to Mecca during the fasting month of *Ramadan* for this most holy ritual. Mecca is off limits to non-Muslims.

MOUNT FUJI, JAPAN

Pilgrims climb Mount Fuji—thought to be the home of many deities—during the night, to arrive at the summit at dawn.

MOUNT KAILASH, TIBET

Followers of three religions, Buddhism, Hinduism, and Tibetan Bon, undertake pilgrimages to this sacred mountain, where they circumambulate the thirty-mile trail around the base of the mountain up to thirteen times. During this meditative journey they leave behind their old selves so they can return home renewed.

CANTERBURY, ENGLAND

This sacred site in southern England was the destination of Chaucer's pilgrims in *The Canterbury Tales*. Canterbury is the resting place of Saint Thomas à Beckett, who was martyred by the knights of King Henry II in 1170. Since then, pilgrims have traveled here to encounter the spiritual powers of the Saint's relics.

BENARES, INDIA

Hindu pilgrims journey to the banks of the Ganges River—believed to be the divine essence of Shiva—to bathe in its purifying waters. It is also the place where many Hindus go to die.

CROAGH PATRICK, IRELAND

The Reek is the most sacred mountain in Ireland, and has been a place of pilgrimage since 44 C.E., when Saint Patrick spent the forty days of Lent at its peak while on a mission to convert pagans to Christianity. Some 60,000 pilgrims make the trek to the summit, some in bare feet, on Reek Sunday, the last Sunday in July.

God wants the heart.

—TALMUD

Making Travel Sacred

Where Are You Called?

What do you seek? What do you hold sacred? My inner compass repeatedly points me to the southwestern United States—a place I am called to return to like a migrating bird when my soul needs a change in climate. Is there a place that beckons you? Do you have recurring dreams of canyon walls? Have you been seeing the Parthenon on billboards, magazine covers, and travel channel specials? Perhaps you have had a fascination with the pyramids since you were eight-years old and long to touch the paws of the Sphinx. The road can persistently whisper to you or ardently beckon you when you least expect it. Either way, you feel the call echoing in a place deep inside yourself. When the call comes, answer it.

Preparing for Departure

Take time before your departure to reflect upon the purpose of your journey. Learn as much about the soul of your destination as you can. Don't limit your research to guidebooks: Read that culture's history, literature, and poetry; study the geography and geology. Doing so may help you to discover the nooks and crannies of experience that are off the beaten tourist track. Also, pack with intention. Whenever I prepare to travel, as my departure draws near, I start to collect items that I want to take on my journey. This serves both a practical and a spiritual purpose. My collection of travel items—an altar of sorts to my impending journey—invites me to ponder my intentions for the trip each time I add something.

The Journey

Traveling away from the familiarity of our everyday lives can help us discover something about ourselves and our world. When we travel with anticipation and joy, the journey can transform us. No matter what the purpose of your trip, take time to meander through and linger at the places you visit. Listen to the voices of the road, touch the temple steps, and find something familiar in the strange or something strange in the familiar. Allow yourself to feel the *anima loci*, or spirit of place. Keep a journal, sketch, and photograph, but never at the cost of really connecting with where you are. Finally, some of the best experiences on the road come from happenstance, so try not to have every moment of your journey planned, and allow for serendipity.

When Problems Arise

When everything on a journey goes exactly as planned, we may feel lucky or that the "travel gods" have been kind. But when nothing unexpected or challenging happens to us—emotionally, physically, or spiritually—there are few chances to test ourselves. Luckily, things don't always happen according to plan, so we often do receive the opportunity to make discoveries and learn. A crowded park, missed train, canceled excursion, or a "closed for the day" sign can become a detour that affords you an opportunity for real surprise and discovery.

Returning Home

What did you discover on your journey? It often takes time to discern the meaning of your travels. You might return with nothing more than an inkling that you were changed, or you might know exactly what the journey brought you. Either way, trust that the pilgrimage brought you closer to your own heart and that the sacred encounters you sought and found will in some way change your life.

Unless you leave room for serendipity, how can the divine enter in? The beginning of the adventure of finding yourself is to lose your way.

—Joseph Campbell

I AM CONVINCED THAT PILGRIMAGE
is still a bona fide spirit-renewing ritual.
But I also believe in pilgrimage as a
powerful metaphor for any journey with the
purpose of finding something
that matters deeply to the traveler.
With a deepening of focus, keen preparation,
attention to the path below our feet, and
respect for the destination at hand, it is
possible to transform even the most ordinary
trip into a sacred journey, a pilgrimage.

—*Phil Cousineau*

Resources: Books and Organizations

BOOKS
General
Campbell, Joseph. *Historical Atlas of World Mythology, Volume I: The Way of the Animal Powers*. New York: Harper and Row, 1988.
Campbell, Joseph. *Creative Mythology: The Masks of God*. New York: Arkana Books, a division of Penguin Books, 1991.
Fox, Matthew. *One River, Many Wells*. New York: Jeremy P. Tarcher/Putnam, 2000.
Hanh, Thich Nhat, Compiled by Jack Lawlor. *Friends on the Path: Living Spiritual Communities*. Berkeley, California: Parallax Press, 2002.
Levoy, Gregg. *Callings: Finding and Following an Authentic Life*. New York: Three Rivers Press, 1997.
Moore, Thomas. *The Soul's Religion: Cultivating a Profoundly Spiritual Way of Life*. New York: Perennial, an Imprint of HarperCollins Publishers, 2002.
Salzberg, Sharon. *Faith: Trusting Your Own Deepest Experience*. New York: Riverhead Books, A Member of Penguin Putnam, Inc., 2002.
Sargent, Denny. *Global Ritualism: Myth & Magic Around the World*. St. Paul, Minnesota: Llewellyn Publications, 1994.
Smith, Huston. *Why Religion Matters: The Fate of the Human Spirit in an Age of Disbelief*. San Francisco: HarperSanFrancisco, 2001.
Zaleski, Philip and Paul Kaufman. *Gifts of the Spirit: Living the Wisdom of the Great Religious Traditions*. San Francisco: HarperSanFrancisco, 1997.

Chapter One: At the Threshold Between Heaven and Earth: Altars
Chester, Laura. *Holy Personal: Looking for Small Private Places of Worship*. Bloomington, Indiana: Indiana University Press, 2000.
Linn, Denise. *Altars: Bringing Sacred Shrines into Your Everyday Life*. New York: The Ballantine Publishing Group, 1999.
McMann, Jean. *Alters and Icons: Sacred Spaces in Everyday Life*. San Francisco: Chronicle Books, 1998.

Chapter Two: Sanctuary in Smoke: Smudging with Sage
Kavasch, E. Barrie and Baar, Karen. *American Indian Healing Arts: Herbs, Rituals, and Remedies for Season of Life*. New York: Bantam Books, 1999.
Morita, Kiyoko. *The Book of Incense: Enjoying the Traditional Art of Japanese Scents*. Tokyo, Japan: Kodansha International Ltd., 1992.
Fischer-Rizzi, Susanne. *The Complete Incense Book*. New York: Sterling Publishing Co. Inc., 1996.

Chapter Three: Between Darkness and Light: The Art of Candle Lighting
Matthews, John. *The Winter Solstice*. Wheaton, Illinois: Quest Books Theosophical Publishing House, 1998.
Zajonc, Arthur. *Catching the Light*. Oxford: Oxford University Press, 1993.

Chapter Four: In Rhythm with the Beat of the Universe: Drumming

Campbell, Don, Editor. *Music and Miracles*. Wheaton, Illinois: Quest Books Theosophical Publishing House, 1992.

Hart, Mickey, and Frederick Lieberman. *Planet Drum*. San Francisco: HarperSanFrancisco, 1991.

McCarthy Draper, Maureen. *The Nature of Music: Beauty, Sound, and Healing*. New York: Riverhead Books, 2001.

Redmond, Layne. *When the Drummers Were Women: A Spiritual History of Rhythm*. New York: Three Rivers Press, 1997.

Chapter Five: Returning to the Source: A Ritual Bath

Ryman, Daniele. *Aromatherapy: The Complete Guide to Plant and Flower Essences for Health and Beauty*. New York: Bantam Books, 1991.

Worwood, Valerie Ann. *The Complete Book of Essential Oils & Aromatherapy*. San Rafael, California: New World Library, 1991.

Chapter Six: Finding One's Center: Meditation with Mandalas

Arguelles, Jose and Miriam. *Mandala*. Boulder, Colorado: Shambhala Publications, Inc., 1972.

Cornell, Judith. *Mandala: Luminous Symbols for Healing*. Wheaton, Illinois: Quest Books Theosophical Publishing House, 1994.

Fincher, Susanne F. *Creating Mandalas: for Insight, Healing, and Self-Expression*. Boston: Shambhala Publications, Inc., 1991.

Jung, C.J. *Jung on Active Imagination*. Princeton, New Jersey: Princeton University Press, 1963.

Jung, C.J. Translated by R.F.C. Hull. *Mandala Symbolism*. Princeton, New Jersey: Princeton University Press, 1959.

Chapter Seven: The Greatness of Little Things: The Way of Tea

Okakura, Kakuzo. *The Book of Tea*. Boston, Massachusetts: Shambhala Publications, Inc., 1993.

Scott, Anne. *Serving Fire: Food for Thought, Body, and Soul*. Berkeley, California: Celestial Arts Publishing, 1994.

Lao Tsu, *Tao te Ching*. New York: Vintage Books, a division of Random House, 1972.

Chapter Eight: Unfolding Mindfulness: Folding One Thousand Cranes

Lafosse, Michael G. *Origami: Masterworks of Paper Folding*. Gloucester, Massachusetts: Rockport Publishers, Inc., 2000.

Suzuki, D. T. *The Zen Doctrine of No-Mind*. York Beach, Maine: Weiser Books, 1972.

Chapter Nine: Putting Our Hearts in Order: Zen Rock Gardens

Borja, Erik. *Zen Gardens*. London, England: Seven Dials, Cassell & Co., 1999.

Maezumi, Taizan and Bernie Glassman, Eds. *On Zen Practice: Body, Breath, Mind*. Boston: Wisdom Publications, 2002.

Murray, Elizabeth. *Cultivating Sacred Space: Gardening for the Soul*. San Francisco: Pomegranate Press, 1997.

Rudloe, Anne. *Butterflies on a Sea Wind: Beginning Zen*. Kansas City, Missouri: Andrews McMeel Publishing, 2002.

Steger, Manfred B. and Perle Besserman. *Grassroots Zen*. Boston: Tuttle, 2001.

Chapter Ten: Coming Full Circle: Walking a Labyrinth

Curry, Helen. *The Way of the Labyrinth: A Powerful Meditation for Everyday Life*. New York: Penguin Compass, 2000.

Kern, Hermann. *Through the Labyrinth*. Munich, Germany: Prestel Verlag, 2000.

Chapter Eleven: Dispatching Prayer: The Andean Despacho

Wilcox, Joan Parisi. *Keepers of the Ancient Knowledge: The Mystical World of the Q'ero Indians of Peru*. Boston: Element Books, Inc., 1999.

Chapter Twelve: Prayer in Motion: Prayer Flags

Lorne Ladner. *Wheel of Great Compassion: The Practice of the Prayer Wheel in Tibetan Buddhism*. Boston: Wisdom Publications, 2000.

Rinpoche, Dagyab. *Buddhist Symbols in Tibetan Culture*. Boston: Wisdom Publications, 1995.

Chapter Thirteen: The Art of Impermanence: Painting with Sand

Farrer-Halls, Gill. *The Illustrated Encyclopedia of Buddhist Wisdom: A Complete Introduction to the Principles and Practices of Buddhism*. Wheaton, Illinois: Quest Books Theosophical Publishing House, 2000.

Mullin, Glen and Andy Weber. *The Mystical Arts of Tibet*. Atlanta: Long Street Press, 1996.

Tibetan Nyingma Meditation Center. *Sacred Art of Tibet*. Berkeley, California: Dharma Publishing, 1972.

Chapter Fourteen: Seeking What the Heart Holds Sacred: Pilgrimage

Coelho, Paul. *The Alchemist: A Fable About Following Your Dream*. New York: HarperCollins Publishers, 1993.

Cousineau, Phil. *The Art of Pilgrimage: The Seeker's Guide to Making Travel Sacred*. Berkeley, California: Conari Press, 1998.

Yeadon, David. *The Way of the Wanderer: Discover Your True Self Through Travel*. San Francisco: Travelers' Tales, 2001.

Organizations and Sources

C. G. Jung Institute, Boston: 36 Newbury Street (3rd floor), Boston, MA 02116-3201. The C. G. Jung Institute sponsors evening and weekend seminars and lectures on a variety of subjects related to the unconscious, dreaming, myth, ritual, imagination, and creativity. Workshops on the mandala are occasionally offered.

Drepung Loseling Monastery, Inc. 2092 Vista Dale Court, Atlanta, GA 30084. www.drepung.org. Their cultural support organization—Mystical Arts of Tibet—offers tours that promote artistic activities of Tibet and the Drepung Loseling Monastery.

Kaji Aso Studio, Institute for the Arts: 40 St. Stephen Street, Boston, MA 02115. Kaji Aso Studio offers courses in visual arts, music, poetry, philosophy, and Japanese culture. Kaji Aso Studio's "House of Flower Wind" is Boston's first Tea House. Special reservations can be made to participate in the Tea Ceremony. Apprenticeships in the study of the Tea Ceremony are available.

Labyrinthos, 53 Thundersley Grove, Thundersley, Essex SS7 3EB, England, U.K. A labyrinth resource center.

Origamido Studio, 63 Wingate Street, Haverhill, MA 01832. www.origamido.com. Origamido offers classes and workshops in origami and other paper arts. They also feature a gallery of fine art and sell books and supplies.

Sacred and Folk Gallery, 1072 Washington Street, Gloucester, MA 01930. www.sacredandfolk.com. Sacred and Folk features an ever-changing collection of sacred objects from all over the world.

Saint Andrew's Church, 135 Lafayette Street, Marblehead, MA, 01945: St. Andrew's has a small outdoor labyrinth, which is open to the public.

Taos Spirit Bundles, P.O. Box 286, Arroyo Seco, NM 87514. A great source for smudge sticks.

Ten Thousand Waves Japanese Health Spa, P.O. Box 10200, Santa Fe, NM 87504. www.tenthousandwaves.com. Ten Thousand Waves offers a Japanese-style bathing experience, as well as aquatic massage and many other spa services. Lodging is available.

The Prairie Labyrinth: c/o Toby Evans: toby@homeisp.com. The Prairie Labyrinth provides opportunities to walk labyrinths that are created by cutting into seasonal grasses in the prarie. Individuals or groups can e-mail to set up an appointment to visit.

Veriditas, c/o Grace Cathedral, 1100 California Street, San Francisco, CA 94108. www.gracecathedral.org. Veriditas is considered "the voice of the labyrinth movement," and offers a variety of labyrinth-related resources.

Picture Credits

Corel (Copyright © 2003 Corel Professional Photos): 14, 15, 17, 22, 23, 24, 35, 41, 48, 54, 56, 72, 73, 79, 105, 111, 115, 116, 120, 121, 122, 123, 138, 139, 152, 153, 155, 160, 161, 168, 178, 179, 182

Toby Evans (© Toby Evans and the Prairie Labyrinth): 128, 135

Laura Kaparoff (courtesy of Dawes Arboretum): 114

Michael LaFosse: Paper Crane Drawing, 101 and 110

Eileen London: 12 ("Heart and Hand"), 44, 65, 100 ("Unfolding Mindfulness"), 104, 140 ("Despacho"), 142, 143, 148 ("Mountain"), 162 ("Impermanence"), 176 ("Pilgrimage"), 180, 181

Eileen London and Belinda Recio: 42 ("Between Darkness and Light"), 150 ("Windhorse")

Kristin Mills: 83, 103, 157-158 (prayer flags), 159

Mystical Arts of Tibet (© Mystical Arts of Tibet): 164, 165

NASA and the Hubble Heritage Team (STScI / AURA): 51, 61

Planet Art: 64, 102

Belinda Recio: v, vi, 18, 19, 20 ("Threshold"), 27, 28, 29, 30, 32("Entrainment"), 37, 40, 46, 50, 52 ("Returning to the Source"), 55, 59, 60, 62, 66, 68, 74 ("Sri Yantra"), 78 ("The Still Point"), 80 ("Mica Mandala"), 81, 85, 86, 88 ("The Greatness of Little Things"), 104, 112 ("Hearts in Order"), 124 ("Coming Full Circle"), 126, 127, 146, 147, 149, 166, 167, 173, 174, 180, 181, 187

Susan Weeks: 93, 98

Jeff Saward / Labyrinthos (Copyright © 2003 Jeff Saward / Labyrinthos): 137

US Bureau of Ethnology: 25

Eric Workman: 16, 23, 25, 26, 27, 31, 34, 36, 37, 38, 39, 45, 47, 48, 58, 59, 64, 67, 70, 71, 76, 81, 87, 90, 91, 92, 94, 95, 96, 97, 99, 106, 107, 108, 109, 117, 118, 119, 129, 130, 131, 132, 136, 144, 145, 146, 154, 155, 156, 157, 158, 170, 171, 172, 175, 184, 185

Photographs appearing on the following pages were taken courtesy of Stephanie Hobart, Sacred and Folk Gallery, Gloucester, MA: 23, 25, 26, 28, 29

Photographs appearing on the following pages were taken courtesy of Kaji Aso Institute for the Arts, Boston, MA: 90, 91, 92, 93, 94, 95

Photographs appearing on the following pages were taken courtesy of St. Andrew's Episcopal Church, Marblehead, MA: 47, 64

Photographs appearing on the following pages were taken courtesy of Ten Thousand Waves, Santa Fe, NM: vi, 28, 65, 66, 68

Photograph on page 38 taken courtesy of Taos Spirit Bundles, Arroyo Seco, NM

Calligraphy appearing in collage on page 88 is courtesy of Kaji Aso.

Loving-kindness Meditation
Meditations to Help You Love Yourself, Love Others,
and Create More Love and Peace in the World

By Bill Scheffel of the Naropa University
ISBN: 1-59233-036-3
$17.00 (£10.99)
Hardcover; 96 pages
Available wherever books are sold

Loving-kindness is an attitude of generosity and compassion toward yourself, toward others, and toward the earth.

Loving-kindness is not a feeling; it's an attitude, a practice. Learn how to practice the art of loving-kindness meditation through evocative images and beautiful poems, blessings, and prayers.

The five steps of loving-kindness meditation:
• *Love yourself*—You must first extend compassion, love, and generosity to yourself.
• *Love your friends*—Meditate on what you love about them.
• *Love a neutral person*—Send good wishes to the mailman or checkout clerk.
• *Love an enemy*—Release the desire for revenge and wish them well.
• *Love the world*—Extend your loving-kindness to the universe.

About the Author
Bill Scheffel is a poet and professor of creative writing and meditation at the Naropa University in Boulder, Colorado. Bill's works include poetry, prose-poetry, and short prose essays. He has read his poetry on National Public Radio and published in numerous literary magazines. Aside from his classes at Naropa, Bill also runs writing workshops in throughout the United States.

Collage for the Soul
Expressing Hopes and Dreams Through Art

By Holly Harrison and Paula Grasdal
ISBN: 1-56496-962-2
$21.95 (£12.99)
Paperback; 136 pages
Available wherever books are sold

A workbook for personal and artistic growth, *Collage for the Soul* will take readers on an interactive journey that will inspire their own creative pursuits. With a focus on artistic process using a variety of techniques, each project not only provides step-by-step instructions but also encourages personal exploration.

The process of making collage transforms the creator just as it recycles and reimagines the found materials used in its creation. Authors Grasdal and Harrison discuss the ideas and themes behind self-expression and creativity, highlighting how we can explore our relationships through art, the ways to see and present nature, and what goes into the making of a visual memoir. They also provide the reader with information on symbols and their meanings—gleaned from many cultures, as well as from art, history, literature, science and nature.

Collage for the Soul presents exercises designed to stimulate ideas and overcome creative blocks. You'll also find comprehensive information about using a variety of collage formats, such as encaustic, found and handmade papers, fabrics, assemblage, and mixed-media collage.

• Includes 26 projects from well-known collage artists, including Nina Bagley, Ann Baldwin, Karen Michel, Lynne Perrella, Deborah Putnoi, Judi Riesch, and Olivia Thomas.
• Each project is accompanied by directions that focus on thematic content, assembling materials, getting started, and using techniques such as photo transfer, gold leaf, encaustic, assemblage, photo montage, computer collage, fabris collage, cast-paper-pulp collage, tissue paper collage, decoupage, painting and printing on paper, working with water-soluble oil pastels, frottage, texturing or altering paper, and altering books.
• Provides and artist's gallery of work by top collage artists, offering inspiration and demonstrating the many ways collage can be used to express ideas and explore personal issues.
• Special sidebars from professional artists provide specific exercises for overcoming creative blocks.

About the Authors
Holly Harrison is a freelance writer and editor. Her first craft book, *Angel Crafts: Graceful Gifts, Inspired Designs*, was published by Rockport Publishers in April 2002. She has also contributed to numerous magazines, including *Metropolitan Home*. She lives in Concord, Massachusetts.

Paula Grasdal is a printmaker and mixed-media artist living in the Seattle area. She has contributed to several other Rockport books, including *Angel Crafts: Graceful Gifts, Inspired Designs*, *The Crafter's Project Book*, and *Making Shadow Boxes and Shrines*. Her work has been exhibited in galleries in the U.S. and Canada.